Strength Becomes You

Doubt to Confidence: Create Your Desired Life

Kathleen Quinton

Library of Congress Control Number: 2021917059

Publisher's Cataloging-In-Publication Data
(Prepared by The Donohue Group, Inc.)

Names: Quinton, Kathleen, author.

Title: Strength becomes you : doubt to confidence : create your desired life / Kathleen Quinton.

Description: First edition. | Marlborough, Massachusetts : Quintessential Productions, [2021] | "Segments of this book have been previously published in: Question Your Thoughts - Empower Your Life." | Includes bibliographical references and index.

Identifiers: ISBN 9781733706766 (softcover) | ISBN 9781733706773 (ebook)

Subjects: LCSH: Self-confidence. | Self-actualization (Psychology) | Belief and doubt. | LCGFT: Self-help publications.

Classification: LCC BF575.S39 S77 2021 (print) | LCC BF575.S39 (ebook) | DDC 158.1--dc23

Contents

Who is this book for?

This book is for you if:

- You're tired of not feeling good enough.
- You feel blocked.
- You over-prepare.
- You find that perfectionism is a compulsion.
- You unconsciously push your common sense to the curb.
- You can't quite "tie the bow" on a project.
- You're going in circles.
- You feel a void.
- You find self-love to be an alien belief.
- You fear success.
- You fear failure.
- You think the "good life" is for everyone else (and maybe it is—perhaps a *fantastic* life is the one for you!).

Looking for strategies to consciously change your thought patterns? I believe this book will help you to optimize your innate strengths to catapult you into your amazing life.

Dedication

This book is dedicated to you, the reader, the dreamer, the mighty doer, the person that persists beyond all justification—kept afloat by uncovering and answering the call from within.

Toss a stone into a pond, and it will create a myriad of ripples. As the stone breaks through the water, a natural expansion occurs that accommodates the stone seamlessly. The water's surface expands outward in perfect circular patterns that make **changes** even as the stone flawlessly becomes one with its new environment.

"Progress is not possible without change,
and those that cannot change their
minds cannot change anything."

–George Bernard Shaw

Introduction

Welcome! This is a book for those of you who may have forgotten that you are good enough.

Whether you want to have better relationships, succeed in business, or believe in your talents and follow your dreams, it all starts with you! The journey begins with the thoughts you have, the questions you ask yourself, the clarity you attain, and the choices that you make.

> *What if you are already enough despite your failures, personal history, and current circumstances and can do anything? What if you could release the negativity that is holding you back and live the life of your dreams? What will it take for you to accept this as truth—to your core?*

You have but one life, and it becomes so darn painful not to grow and reach your full potential! You cannot afford to sit still and let time continue to pass you by.

Those limiting beliefs we carry can wear us down. It's time to question those thoughts and start asking,

"Why not me?"

With clear thinking comes belief and strategic action. You are meant to reach your full potential. Let's find the strength within you to make that happen!

I know the fear of stepping outside of your comfort zone and what it takes to overcome it. I did my work, read the books, attended the seminars, watched, listened, learned, and became a certified life coach. I still do my work because this is what I love and am compelled to do. I am incredibly passionate about uplifting people's perspectives and enticing them out of a cycle of negativity. My goal for this book is to inspire and empower you to take years off your climb to personal and professional success.

Regardless of your past or current circumstances, or your age, you can start a new journey today. I will share with you how to build your confidence to trust in yourself and feel motivated to test the empowerment waters wherever they may be.

This book is the start of your positive coaching journey. Absorb the processes, modalities, and stories of others' successes and accomplishments so that they can inspire your own growth. Like a coach meeting a client for the first time, this book is written to meet you, the reader, where you are now and to be a partner in making the shift toward a desired new state of mind and being!

Perhaps the most important thing that you will take away from this book is an increase in emotional strength and depth so that when you tell yourself an untruth—like, "I am not good enough."—you will no longer stand for it. Not for one more minute.

That is confidence at its best! It is freeing and un-limiting in its gifts. As you reach each new milestone in life, this new-found confidence will catapult you to upgrade your circumstances repeatedly. You'll be able to identify when you get off track and then quickly pivot yourself to get back on track sooner. Happiness, passion, and confidence can become your norm.

Why exactly did I write this book? To help you make a conscious choice to live a life of purpose with fearless passion and joy so that on reckoning day, your regrets will be few.

Imagine what you can do when you remove all doubt and allow your uniqueness to shine through.

Cheers,

Kathy

Chapter 1

COACHING: A PARTNERSHIP TO GROWTH AND SUCCESS

Introduction

I'm a life coach. After receiving my first certification, I still had the mindset of "I'm not ready to be a coach yet." So, I continued to extend my qualifications by seeking new skills and additional certifications to supplement my resume. My clients were doing fantastically, but I still lacked confidence in myself. I kept an escape route—a loophole or a way back to the business world if needed. All the while, I continued coaching clients and felt a disconnect with my former profession, expertise and qualifications. One foot in the coaching world, and the other foot still tiptoeing in places it didn't quite fit anymore.

My clients began to make positive changes. They looked healthier, stood taller. They owned their space in this world, smiled more, and reached for more challenging projects. They began to believe in their power again and to make things happen. They understood that failure was only a step towards their subsequent success. They stopped seeing limits; instead, they saw opportunities. My clients now viewed failing as the beginning, not the end, of their journey—a perspective different from what it once had been.

Their feedback and results buoyed me. While utilizing both my newly acquired skills and my life experiences, my confidence grew. My work began to feel like home. I acknowledged that I am a coach, and sometimes a coach's coach and a coaching client. Additionally, I'm a writer and I am very open to self-improvement. I had to burn the bridge and get behind my new profession! I do not limit myself at all. Coaching and writing are a good fit for me. This book is my way of sharing what I've learned to help more people become stronger individuals.

It is not a sign of weakness to work with a coach or mentor, read self-help books, or consciously try to grow! Instead, it is a clear sign of forward movement.

In sports, we see the profound benefits of coaching. Elite athletes rely on their coaches' support throughout their careers. A coach is a growth and success partner. You can expect to find a little bit of mentor, partner, friend, lie detector, exposer of potential, and holder of dreams in your coach. It may sound fanciful unless you have experienced the process. It is normal—and often valuable—to have a coach.

I have worked with various coaches over several years,

and I have not looked back—except in gratitude. The clarity and beliefs I gained produced a high return in terms of reclaiming my life. Being coached was far better than waiting one more minute for life to kick into gear. The only thing worse than being stuck is being stuck one day longer than you need to be.

A life coach's job is to support you in the gap between your current state, which is where you are now, and your desired state, where you want to be. Thus, coaches meet clients where they are and hold their space for them until they reach the goals that they have set for themselves.

When a coach works with you, you become partners. This partnership means that together the coach and client unpack the old and make room for the new. Unpacking can be questioning deeply set thoughts that no longer serve you. It can also involve finding what is suitable for you today or learning the real nuts and bolts of what you need to concentrate on to grow. Once we get to a good-feeling place, then we set our sights on a compelling future.

When limiting thoughts are unpacked, you open space to claim what you want. Action steps soon follow; moving forward becomes more natural than ever before because:

- You know what you want.
- You'll be free from limiting thoughts and can generate the energy and passion for pursuing your desired state.

- Each new effort is accompanied by more confidence and strength, allowing you to reach even further. This becomes easy once you do the hard work.

Results come via strategic questions and processes, life experiences, instincts, research, accountability, and action. Never underestimate the power of having an accountability partner, like a coach, who focuses solely on their client's well-being and goals.

So, let's do this!

Reflection

I still quote my life coach today; I remember our first meeting like it was yesterday. She told me that the three following questions were life-changing, and if I could already answer them, I wouldn't need her!

They were:

1. What do you want?
2. What is the truth?
3. What is the worst thing that can happen?

Well, those questions may not have changed my life that day, but I certainly understand them thoroughly today.

Let's break them down.

1. What do you want?

Knowing what we want gives us clarity. What happens when we are sure about something? We act. We are confident about what our next steps should be. We do not doubt ourselves. We plot, plan, and execute. This kind of knowledge brings forth a variety of strengths.

2. What is the truth?

Could it be true that we are good enough? Kind, smart, capable, and robust enough? That we all deserve a satisfying life? If you feel otherwise, where did those other thoughts come from? Perhaps they benefitted you at one time? When we understand where those thoughts came from, we are more than capable of dealing with them. We discover, plan, and execute.

3. What is the worst that can happen?

Is failing the worst thing that can happen? Will it lead to a major disaster, a minor setback, embarrassment, or just a lesson? Or is the worst thing never to have tried in the first place? Which path is apt to bring you the most regret or happiness?

Maturity should be our life's goal. Accepting responsibility for our thoughts and actions brings us to this place. Acknowledging our failures without excuses or blame is the only way that we will mature.

This C.S. Lewis quote below resonates with me as it relates directly to the above three questions. C.S. Lewis shares with us about what gifts maturity can bring.

*When I was ten, I read fairy tales in
secret and would have been ashamed
if I had been found doing so. Now that
I am fifty, I read them openly. When
I became a "mature" man, I put away
childish things, including the "fear" of
childishness and the desire to grow up.*

—C.S. LEWIS

What did he want? To read fairy tales.

What was the truth? He hid as he read fairy tales.

What was the worst that could happen? Feelings of embarrassment and shame.

When he put away childish thoughts, he could freely be his authentic self. He could do all that he wanted— even childish things—without concern about critique. Maturity is a beautiful thing. It allows you to be yourself without fear. This Strength Becomes You!

Coach versus Therapist

Both a coach and therapist work strategically to help empower your life. But a coach is not the same as a therapist. Therapists are more interested in your past. They can help heal your long-held wounds and some diagnose personality disorders. If you are in a constant state of emotional pain, have thoughts of suicide or self-harm, or past circumstances continue to interfere with your growth, then I would highly recommend that you find a competent therapist.

A coach is more interested in meeting you where you are today and helping you reach your desired state. Healing can also happen organically through coaching. Coaches work to shine a light on what is true today—always keeping our client's wellness and future goals in mind.

My reason for explaining the difference between therapy and coaching is simply because people ask—I want to help the reader to clarify how to make the best choice between the two for their optimal growth. Your life is calling, after all!

Going Deeper

What can you do to help yourself progress? Throughout this book, I'll be giving you action points and exercises to guide you on your coaching journey.

The first is to figure out where you want to go.

Think of those three key questions:

- *What do you want?* If you could live life in any way you desire, what would yours look like?

- *What is the truth?* What is your life like now? What do you feel is holding you back? What can you let go of?

- *What is the worst that could happen?* What

are you afraid of that might occur if you attempt to grow, change, and reach for all you want?

Exercise

Write the three questions and answers on a piece of paper or revisit them every time you feel yourself wavering and uncertain about moving forward.

- What do you want?
- What is the truth?
- What's the worst that could happen?

In upcoming chapters, we'll explore the power that comes from knowing what you want in more depth.

Summary

A life coach can help you move on in your life by working with you to establish what you want while keeping an eye on your future.

If you feel that your past needs closer examination, you might prefer to work with a therapist who can help put you on the path to healing. If you're already on that path, then a life coach and this book can help you progress faster.

Chapter 2

CLARITY

Introduction

Do you believe in "Aha!" moments? Pivotal life-changing events? Experiences so deeply felt they jolt an awareness, wake us up, or bring clarity instantly? Are you confident that ***the teacher, words, or experience will come when the pupil is ready?*** Here we examine a story about a deeply embedded thought and its outcome of developing new perspectives.

A Brother's Story

John was born sensitive. He grew up in abuse, neglect, and dysfunction. His bloodline had seen many die young. He was prone to addiction because many relatives before him had been addicts and died young. Sadly, as it turned out, John did die, even younger than all those before him.

Since John was so young, his death shocked everyone

but his family. The shock his family felt was more of the visceral variety. They had witnessed and lived through the ravages John endured. On some level, they knew that time was not on his side. On another, they deluded themselves, because how can someone so young die from alcoholism?

The harm caused by the alcohol alone was so advanced for someone of his age that his condition became of significant interest to the medical community. The doctors had him filmed in the hospital. Many years after John passed away, his brother Frank sought help from a therapist to get clear about his own life. The discussion kept circling back to his brother John. Frank shared with his therapist that a history of addiction went back for generations in his family. He could prove this point explicitly as he knew the stories and names of all those it had enveloped in each generation of his family thus far.

The therapist listened well, as good therapists do, and asked a few pointed questions. Then, she shared a story about raising her sensitive child and how she had to be both patient and diligent in guiding her child through life's challenges. Further, she acknowledged that being a trained therapist helped her to support her sensitive son to negotiate through his childhood obstacles.

Frank tensed; he knew that his therapist was about to make a point, and she did. She asked Frank, "What do you suppose would have happened to my sensitive son had he grown up with your family?"

Without a blink of an eye, Frank said, "He would have

died an alcoholic at the age of twenty-six." Boom.

Time stood still for Frank as he absorbed this understanding. Thousands of fragments of his former confusing thoughts fell into place. In an instant he was no longer a huge believer in people being "prone" to becoming an alcoholic. Frank now realized that this had been a mere theory, passed down through generations, that he had *locked* in his *mind* as a *truth* without bothering to question it.

With that one story and that one strategic question, CLARITY came calling, allowing Frank to make a life altering shift in his perspective.

> *Clarity was the key. It brought an awareness to Frank's life, saving future generations from a cycle of dysfunction. His beliefs transformed into a knowing.*

Clarity Affects Nurturing

Part of our life's work is to make sense of the noise circulating in our minds. This especially includes unraveling the untruths and unhealthy thought patterns that some of us may have accepted along the way.

Frank was told that his brother died because he was prone to be an addict. Unfortunately, Frank and his parents believed this and had never examined that premise further. (It was sure better than them taking some of the responsibility.) Notice how this concept doesn't acknowledge that John had too many wounds to process alone, that he felt unworthy, or that he was self-medicating. Are these more likely some traits that alcoholics are prone to have?

Instead, they believed the effortless answer of "It was meant to be."

Now Frank had a new and clear path of understanding. In truth, he knew that his brother John was more genetically prone to be kind and easy-going. He was known to be a sensitive kid who was funny and happened to be right-handed, tall with thick wavy brown hair and blue eyes.

Is this the nature versus nurture conversation? And if so, can a lack of nurturing ruin a life?

Can we reverse-engineer John's childhood and find out?

Thankfully, we continue to evolve. At one time, many hardships were considered acceptable for children to endure. Children appear to be very resilient. With love and their needs being met, yes, that is true, but how far on a dysfunctional journey can they bounce back?

Adults haven't always considered that children have needs that are important for their personal development. Food for physical growth, yes, but consciously nurturing personal development was truly a rarity when John was raised. The understanding that children have their little spirits inside of them longing to burst forth was a tenet not often passed down from generation to generation.

The customary view that "children should be seen and not be heard" was (and in many places in the world continues to be) real. Most children are molded and shaped according to what conditioning their parents had or society deems to be important. Consider how much longer it will take a child raised this way to find their unique selves. This style is usually well intentioned and practiced to keep children safe.

Yet John wasn't safe in a dysfunctional and abusive home. A home where parents didn't question their thoughts and behavior. A home where this is how it was, and this is how it will be. A home where conscious growth was not the norm.

I'm convinced that we should "listen to understand." Otherwise, if children—and all people—are unheard, with feelings left unresolved, they will continue to surface repeatedly until they are resolved. Limiting patterns may linger well into adulthood until they are finally examined and understood for what they are: thoughts/feelings, not facts.

Conscious parenting is entering the mainstream. It's an opportunity to appreciate how an upbringing/nurture affects children and adults. Many adults become healed of their negative patterns as they nurture children. We can examine our beliefs to discover what in our conditioning may have hindered us. We can find clarity and overcome unresolved feelings.

In Frank's case, the clarity he found created a stronger foundation for him. He was able to understand what really was and to choose effective ways to resolve negative patterns. He needed this firmer foundation before he could move forward. It was not only enlightening—he also found it freeing.

Sharon's story

Sometimes clarity is more about what you want in life and in recognizing the foundation you already have.

I had the pleasure of coaching Sharon. The first thing that resonated with me about Sharon was her honesty and inner strength. She followed all the rules, lived in a world of "do unto others," and expected the same in return.

The reason she came to coaching was that she felt a lack of appreciation from her employer. She had a history of impeccable reviews and had climbed the ranks of the organization quickly. However, all of that had changed with her most recent performance review. The review mentioned that her leadership skills were lacking; the "proof" was that an employee she was responsible for had become a liability to the organization. With this explanation, Sharon did not receive a raise for the first time and wasn't allowed to share her side of the story. She felt blindsided by those she looked up to; it was a severe blow to her self-esteem.

The back story is that Sharon had an employee in her department who had become a concern. Sharon followed protocol and reached out to both her manager and HR department to share her apprehensions. Unfortunately, no one on her management team validated these concerns, and Sharon's work-life continued as though she hadn't raised a red flag or asked for help.

Eventually, this employee was fired, and the reason was kept confidential, even from Sharon! She worked in a high-security corporate setting, so when someone was removed (e.g., fired), they were summarily escorted from the workplace.

Ultimately, Sharon was held responsible for her employee's actions, even though she had predicted that this employee was a liability from the beginning! She had followed the company guidelines and reported the situation as soon as she sensed it developing.

As we unraveled her work situation, the less-than-favorable review, and this employee's termination, it was clear that Sharon believed that she had become an easy scapegoat for what had occurred in the organization.

Left confused and disheartened, she started to believe that she was the worst manager in the entire organization. Going to work each day became a challenge, and she detested the feeling of resentment that was enveloping her.

However, as the breadwinner at home, Sharon had many financial obligations, and she could not let pride or anger push her to quit her job abruptly. Leaving her position without another one with equal pay and benefits in place was not an option.

We worked on finding some clarity for her—both personally and professionally. What came out of Sharon's clarity session was surprisingly empowering for her. In the daily grind of life, she had forgotten herself and her many strengths. She had already conquered obstacles that few people had ever faced. Sharon may have come to coaching to resolve a work issue, yet the results also led her to become reacquainted with her powerful self!

By nature, "rule-followers" are very honest people. They tend to do their job, climb the next rung of the ladder, and not make any waves. Management loves them because they are not high-maintenance employees, and they get the job done. Rule-followers are not found hanging around in cliques or gossiping—that is not their style. They expect a level and fair playing field. It pays to note that rule-followers tend to be so focused on their mission that they can be easily blindsided.

Life can be a self-fulfilling prophecy: *I really am not good enough; this situation just proves it. Things like this do not happen to successful people. I am such a loser.* And so on.

Our internal dialog about ourselves becomes our set point. If we think we are not good enough, that can become the only level we ever reach. We won't aim higher.

Allow me to clarify this point. The sole reason that anyone may be mistreated is that, on some level, *they allow it.* This is an unhealthy pattern for sure, and like all patterns, it will continue until clarity shines a light on what really is going on, and we stop it! In truth, it is ultimately up to us to decide how we allow others to treat us.

Once Sharon delved a bit deeper and unraveled her life story, I knew that I was working with a resilient and intelligent woman! As a young child, she had immigrated to the United States, learned a new language, absorbed a new culture, lost her father and abusive grandmother, then had to adjust to a new family. She maneuvered through her childhood with great caution and seriously good coping skills.

She grew up, attended college, got married, had children, then got divorced. And this is just some of what had occurred in her life when she found herself unfairly stymied by a false charge at work.

In the hustle and bustle of her life, she took her innate strength, impressive coping skills, and leadership traits for granted. This was because they came easy to her; thus, she discounted them. She also hadn't ever had the time to take stock of all that she has done. Fortunately, that changed!

Sharon became clear about what she wanted and how she expected to be treated at work and in life. Her true nature is to be happy and productive. She works hard and cares hard—a leader by nature! As a well-known and respected community leader, Sharon manages her department, her home and organizes church initiatives. It wasn't until her integrity was questioned and on the line that Sharon became compelled to check in on her belief systems. It turned out that it was time to let go of some old stories that she'd been carrying with her for years.

When we got to the heart of the matter, she needed to look at herself honestly—at her excellent work ethic along with a myriad of other accomplishments—and to allow herself to celebrate her successes. She had to consciously acknowledge her strengths and accomplishments in her life.

People and situations will not rock your world when you know yourself and what you want, and are good with who you are. Thankfully, she had a lot of resources to pull from. Sharon quickly started to believe in herself again. She was equally quick to make some strategic and meaningful changes at work and in other areas of her life. (Quick, as in the very next day!)

The changes she made were small at first but were within her comfort level at the time. These POSITIVE changes, along with a new show of confidence, immediately drew a positive response from her staff. The team that she led was thriving!

We can play small at work and in life. We may not want to upset the apple cart or overstep authority, but it is always best to be your authentic self and let your gifts shine. Not only does it permit others to do the same, but you will also be tested less and *treated better*!

The last time we spoke, Sharon led the entire organization in sales for that month. She mentioned to me that many opportunities inside and outside of work are coming her way. She is happier and growing more confident by the day. I often wonder what Sharon's superiors think about her leadership skills now. It is still ironic to me that they ever questioned her leadership abilities. Sometimes human nature forgets the power and energy of honest hardworking people!

Finding clarity can be exciting as well as empowering. It is one of those *rare occurrences* that can have immediate results. At first, Sharon had a difficult time regaining her power. She was more inclined to believe good things about everyone but herself.

However, once she received clarity regarding her power, by recognizing past successes, and reengaging with her innate strengths, great things started to happen. Once you get clear about what you want—right then, in that very moment, it can free you from all the confusion that comes from focusing on what you do not want.

Reflection

Gaining clarity is such a significant accomplishment in and of itself. You will refuse to waste any more of your precious time and energy on what you do not want. It helps you build emotional muscle to begin a concentrated effort on what will benefit you and let you attain your goals.

We become empowered when we focus on our goals. We become happy doing what it takes to attain them because we are aiming for results that we desire. We are a hundred times more likely to act upon and accomplish a goal when we are clear and steadfast, NOT wishy-washy, about what we want!

We hear a lot about being present—not living in the past or focusing too much on tomorrow. Finding clarity is an indispensable step to living in the present while attaining your happiness and success in life.

Everyone has various interests and obligations. Perhaps you may wear too many hats. A good many of us can go through life distracted or even in a state of survival mode. Be honest with yourself—how many distractions have you allowed in your life to stop you from accomplishing your goals?

Our thinking and focus can become so disjointed. It is impossible to complete a project if you don't take the time to focus on it. How many projects and dreams have you left unfinished or behind you simply because you didn't focus on them? Getting clear about what you want becomes essential to your growth and trajectory forward.

We all set standards for our lives at a young age. A lot of these decisions were made unconsciously—almost in passing. Even so, they were definite and decisive decisions at the time. It is almost as though you made a pact with yourself. You have kept it and reached this point. So, what now?

> *Discovering what you **don't** want in life should only be used as knowledge for what you **do** want. Your focus and energy need to be fixed on the positive.*

You might well remember thinking things like, *I want a good life for myself and my family. I want to be a good mother/father. I won't be like them. I will be a person of integrity. I will be fit and healthy. I want to make a lot of money. I want to have a hot fudge sundae every day if I want it!*

It's vitally important to have a clear picture of what you want, and an excellent way to do this is to acknowledge what you do not want! (i.e., *I don't want to struggle from paycheck to paycheck. I want to bring the best of myself to others. I want to earn an excellent salary that allows me to pay my bills, travel that will bring me and others joy, save for retirement, and live a comfortable life.*)

If you are not satisfied with any area of your life, it is time to drop the old ways, tweak your thinking, and consciously create new standards and goals to move onward and upward.

You cannot spend the whole of your life living for that ten- to twenty-one-year-old decision maker. It would be best to accept where you are now, how you have arrived at this point, and make a new plan to move forward.

Life can be busy, especially when there is a lot of noise and confusion going on. Perhaps it is time to remove yourself from that noise and confusion. By gaining focus, you will have a clear path towards accomplishing your goals.

Let's look at clarity from one more perspective.

Have you ever been "in the zone"? There is nothing quite like the kind of synchronicity you can feel when you are doing what you are meant to do or want to do. This is when your skills, thoughts, energy, and passions are aligned, and all is right with the world.

When you have this feeling, you'll know that you are where you are meant to be and doing what you are meant to do. Fear, self-doubt, and shyness fall away when you are working/living within your purpose/calling. When you have this kind of clarity, you are compelled to focus and act.

An example of this alignment is when you are watching a sporting event. I am a New Englander, and New Englanders have had a front-row seat to this phenomenon of being in the zone. We have heard the tales and watched the likes of Celtics legend Larry Bird, Red Sox great Ted Williams, NFL Patriots quarterback Tom Brady, and many more stellar athletes over the years. I can say with some confidence that each coach, owner, and fan knew that the ball should be in those players' hands. The same can be said for the players themselves—of course, they wanted that ball, oh, did they ever. You can bet that they had absolute clarity about what they would do with it!

You can replace the names of these players with other magnificent athletes, musicians/singers, dancers, actors, artists, poets, writers, speakers, or any great achievers that you may know. It becomes magical when focus, practice, skills, experience, and wisdom align.

Going Deeper

Clarity is your truth, and your personal truth will always resonate with you. Securing your buy-in and getting 100 percent behind your conscious decisions is the impetus towards getting to where you want to go.

When you focus your attention on what you want, you become infused with an energy that will compel you towards it. Nothing is better than being clear about what you want in life. Knowing your goal is the first step towards attaining it.

So, let's do this together! Try the exercise below. Take your time with it. If you put your all into it, I promise that you will ignite the spark inside of you—an "aha" moment—and it will set the stage for the next chapters to come.

Exercise

Start by writing down what you don't want in an area of your life on a piece of paper.

You can choose to work on your relationships, health, career, finances, environment, etc. After choosing one, write a detailed description by listing out what exactly you don't want in that area of your life. Once you have completed the "don't want" section, write down what you do want with equal detail in that area of your life instead.

Follow the examples below for a template to set up this list. You can fold a piece of paper in half vertically and list your "don't wants" on the left and your "wants" on the right.

Creating this comparison chart is a crucial step to achieve positive results. When you are finished filling this out, the wants are all you should focus on moving forward. You must know what you do not want—but ONLY for the knowledge that it will give you to move in the direction of what you want.

You can scratch through the "don't want" section, ceremoniously burn that sheet of paper, or tuck it away. Only return to this portion of the chart to remind yourself how far you have come—or to remember why you "want what you want!"

- I don't want…

- I want…

- I don't want…

- I want…

Hopefully, you already feel a sense of knowing come over you as you start to formulate the direction you want to go. With this level of clarity, you can begin to set goals and action steps. You can create a mission statement, a personal tagline, or perhaps a vision board, etc. I recommend staying vigilant and revisiting your goals. It can be so easy to have an "aha" moment and then fold right back into our lives and put the new insight on hold.

We cannot do that any longer—change requires you to MAKE A DECISION to act on these insights now and make them a part of our lives right away.

Review your wants list, and next to them, note any discoveries and breakthroughs you experienced about the power of clarity. What are you clear about? What do you want? Please don't move on to the next chapter without a clear and definite takeaway.

Summary

We must understand what we don't want to gain the *knowledge* it gives us about what we want. Consciously realizing what we do not want is a more expedient way to find clarity about our true desires. Knowing what we want will increase our energy and will lead to a decisive plan to accomplish our goals strategically.

The predictor of future behavior is past behavior. To change your behavior and, therefore, your future, question your thoughts, get clarity, and take the action steps. The tip here is to laser focus on your goals and positive desires in life and move in that direction.

Your wants will become your life map. The next steps will come to light right before you. You'll feel the pull; all you need is to believe in it and go for it. It becomes a journey of knowing—not just a belief for a period of time—but a true knowing. This clarity is your truth, and you cannot unknow what you now know.

When you start to go off course from your goals, stop and remember what you want/know, ground yourself, be decisive, and move on. You don't want to waste a moment of your phenomenal energy on what you do not want. Instead, use this power to create a life that meets your needs, utilizes your talents, fulfills your purpose, and leads you to fulfillment. It takes practice and discipline to stay the course, but it is almost impossible not to stay the course once you've found it.

Chapter 3

GROUNDING

Introduction

Being grounded, centered, or balanced is equally important to gaining clarity. I was torn about which should come first, the clarity or the grounding. Let's say they are like peanut butter and chocolate—they make each other so much better!

That is why I am sharing both superpowers at the beginning of this book. Depending on the client, I can build a case for focusing first on one over the other. If I sense a client is more anxious than confused, I'll work hard to ground them so they will feel a sense of balance and strength.

However, I will never refute that clarity is also critical. I tend to think of it as the grounding of the mind. Without clarity, we cannot bring ourselves to a state of stability. We need the clarity to say to ourselves: okay, stop and get grounded so you can think properly. We use our grounding to regain stability and the ability to remain calm.

> *You are born good enough and worthy; that is part of both the gift and confusion of life. Some can spend their lives looking for what they already have and become ungrounded. Just being born is proof that we belong and are worthy of being here.*

Being grounded helps us to feel balanced and to cultivate self-love. It helps us to be conscious of the here and now. A **grounded** individual does not scatter their forces. A **grounded** individual is solid and deals with things as they are rather than how they wish them to be.

A grounded person still dreams big. They accomplish many of their goals because they are grounded in their sense of self. They do their work, set goals, and take steps to make their dreams a reality. A grounded person is at peace with their body, mind, and spirit in spiritual terms, hence the Clarity and Grounding partnership!

Vicious cycles are typical if you are not grounded. Picture your thoughts as the hamster wheel continuously spinning. A part of you wants to get off, but what then? Can you get hurt by jumping off and changing course? Will others be upset if you do? Will they think less of you if you need to pause, take a break? Will they think of you as weak for not accomplishing anything? Should you care what others think?

Patterns like this can be the rule, and I work with them

often. When my clients have difficulty putting their thoughts into words or feeling emotional and may not want to face a situation, I'll have them change their physiology by standing up, and deliberately ground their bodies. This change alone can work wonders to quickly bring them back to a calm state and a place of clarity. They just needed to feel stable and safe within themselves to focus and find their voice.

Jillian's story

Jillian came to me to find her way out of one of these vicious cycles. She was confused because she kept doing many different things but still felt stuck. Jillian wondered how this was possible if she engaged in so many activities.

She began the coaching process already open, brave, and raring to go. Usually, my clients need to work up to this level of energy and attitude. Not Jillian—she was a believer in the process already. She had known how to get things done in the past, and she knew that she could do it again!

Jillian was a talented woman with all the degrees and certifications to prove it. She was capable, skilled, and full of all this raring-to-go energy, but she was stuck. The only thing I was certain about when we started was that she was going to be fun to work with!

Jillian wanted to end a long-term relationship and find work to support herself. She also had several high-level projects in the works—or even on hold! Her enviable energy was scattered in too many directions. It was as though she had reached a plateau or a "good enough" standard for herself.

As she was waiting to figure out a solution, Jillian worked hard to help others bring their projects to completion. She'd make other people's dreams and wishes her priority.

We created a mental picture of her running around, holding up one of her projects, then another, trying to keep them up in the air so that they would not fall. We would refer to these projects as her magical boxes of unfinished projects. Magical because her projects were highly creative and sophisticated. The problem, though, was that none were successfully completed.

Jillian was dispersing her attention and energy in too many directions. Her significant personal and professional goals were eluding her. It was as though she had opened the door to her creativity and gifts yet didn't know how to tend to them when the wind, rain, and storms of life came her way.

On some level, this may have felt like freedom to Jillian. Soon into coaching, it was apparent that personal freedom was fundamental to her. Perhaps scattering her thoughts fed her free-spirited nature to some degree, giving her a sense of excitement and variety. Could she be deflecting and hiding? Whatever the reason, it ultimately became a roadblock to her sense of security and being fulfilled.

Even a talented free spirit needs to land sometimes. (When we come from a place of clarity and being centered, doors will open to whatever it is that you want to accomplish.) She was experiencing an uncomfortable time. She didn't appear stuck to others because of her many diversions. She could say with honesty, "I am doing this, that, or any other high-level project." Being involved in multiple projects gave her a sense of significance and pride—until she wanted more!

The telltale sign that Jillian was very stuck was because she was not accomplishing her goals. Why was she stuck? Getting balance became a critical step for her to move toward her future success. It was soon clear to both of us that scattering her forces and energy left her feeling more depleted than the completion of one project ever could!

(Throughout this book, we will touch on our life's maps, set points, what we accept as a "good enough" life, our human needs, etc. These beliefs and more can enable our plateauing, resting too long, feeling stuck, and they can even send us into a bit of a tailspin.)

To ground herself, Jillian created a metaphor. She imagined feeling like the massive sturdy redwood tree with its deep roots, and at other times like a majestic mountain, each being able to hold its own no matter what. We visualized how the redwood tree and the mountains are so sturdy and grounded that a gale wind, or any other change, cannot move them from their purpose.

We examined how we can be wholly uprooted (much like Dorothy in *The Wizard of Oz*), and we created a visual of a young tree in a harsh wind being blown around violently. Seeing how every little breeze has the potential to rock a fragile tree—or an ungrounded spirit—careful tending was needed. A fragile tree is not yet sturdy enough to withstand the wind.

Once Jillian saw that she would not lose her creativity and free-spirited nature by being grounded, she was all in. She knew that she wanted to share her gifts with others. The only way to do that was to be clear, conscious and to focus on her goals long enough to accomplish them.

Once she became grounded, she also became stronger—or perhaps she remembered who she was—and that is when the coaching process truly began. Jillian found that she had forgotten her strength as she moved through life.

I still marvel at all the creativity and energy of this one person. Just by understanding the concept of feeling balanced, harnessing her power and gifts, and directing them in a focused way Jillian gained the freedom she always craved. She wanted to feel free and to accomplish her goals. Can she have both?

Reflection

You can ground yourself with your body and your mind. The body is the house of your being. Your thoughts and spirit reside within the body. Yet, many of us go through life, taking our bodies for granted.

Sometimes it is impractical to stand to feel grounded

physically. If that is the case, you can visualize a grounding practice. It can become second nature for you. You will be able to imagine yourself as calm, strong, and grounded in stressful moments. You'll be able to think more logically, even in the most intense situations.

Like Jillian, you can create a metaphor that will help you to feel powerful. Mine is the massive redwood tree. I see the depths of the roots belonging to the earth and the unmovable strength of it.

You may prefer the majesty of a mountain, the sky, the ocean, or something else entirely. It's your choice since it is your visualization. There is something magical about consciously owning your space through your body; it seems to validate us and, most importantly, remind us how we do matter and how very much we do belong.

Feeling this sense of belonging will allow for a more positive response to life's challenges in a peaceful and unemotional way. This is when you can yield positive results and reap what you sow.

Finding yourself in a vicious cycle is not unusual if you are not grounded. If anything, this can be the rule. Many times, we are living more unconsciously, stranded, yet very busy in survival mode. Although we are still getting things done on a high level (lots of things), what is missing?

- Definite Decisions
- Goals
- Strategic Steps

The individuality of people and how they meet their needs can be staggering. Some need to be less like the redwood tree or mountain (rigid and unmoving) and more like water that flows or the young tree that allows its branches to blow freely in the wind. It's about finding a balance that works for you.

What joy is there if we are not growing, thriving, and accomplishing our goals? Once we are cognizant of our core beliefs, purpose, and goals, we are prepared to begin to change.

Jillian's nature reminded me of a firefly, flitting from project to project, job to job, or person to person, never stopping long enough to grow the roots needed to know themselves or their purpose. Perhaps the payoff of not staying with something long enough to reach a result could be to avoid taking responsibility for the outcome? Fear of being judged? Of not being perfect enough?

So, instead, they keep flitting on by as fast as they can.

Jillian and I continue to keep in touch, and we have great laughs with each other. She is happier and continues to gain more confidence in herself and her abilities. She is moving forward, accepting (and completing) new projects that come her way. Jillian has found work; she is living independently and finding her sense of direction. She had always believed in herself—but almost in a careless way. She wanted and was able to attain for herself because she alone can meet her needs. She still runs and flits around...however, now it's done consciously and with purpose.

The last time we spoke, she told me, "I feel like I am still, but I am moving." The *still* resonated with me of her being both grounded and clear; the *moving* spoke to me of her taking action. It indeed was not the vision of someone stuck and going around in unproductive circles.

Going Deeper

Grounding is stabilizing. When you are stable, you can safely challenge your thoughts and empower your ways of thinking. The stabilizing creates a foundation for a more inquisitive mind whose side effects are more confidence. If you list your strengths, you may amaze yourself. Once you know how far you've already come and how many bridges you have already crossed, it encourages more self-esteem. I have clients list their strengths more than once to watch the list grow!

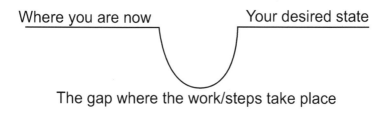

The gap where the work/steps take place

The gap between where you are now and your desired state is where you do the growth work. Being grounded helps you to marshal more resources and maintain the belief required to keep growing. Over time it becomes easier because you continue to gain more skills to supplement your strengths.

Grounding allows you to find the inner space to recharge and to rediscover the spark once again. With this, the second or third attempt at something will never be as hard as the first. Just start towards your goal, and the momentum needed will meet you.

Try being conscious as you change your physiology. Stand tall, hold your head high, push your shoulders back, look people in the eyes, and smile. This is what being grounded looks like. Empowered is what it will feel like.

After reading Chapter Two, you should have a clearer understanding of what you do want. Now add being grounded and balanced to your newfound clarity, and positive changes will start to happen—even today! Knowing how to ground yourself will strengthen you— both in mind and in the body—exponentially. It will help to increase your resolve so you can act on what you want.

Try to think of clarity as an awakening of your truth and grounding as a physical sense of well-being. Can you get a sense of the power that comes with a healthy mind and body?

Why are being grounded and having clarity essential? Without balance and knowing your real worth, you may: over-talk; not speak at all; appear angry, sad, or impatient; make yourself small and wish to disappear— all to the detriment of what you want, not to mention your success in life.

Have you ever been in any of these life situations?

- You jump in and speak when you shouldn't and end up with "meeting regret"?
- You can't think clearly?
- You lose your train of thought?
- You receive unsettling news?
- You're blindsided by a trusted friend or colleague?
- You've gotten fired?
- You've had your car repossessed?
- You win the lottery?

Good, bad, and of course, traumatic events can rock your world. Ask yourself how often you have wished that you could remain calm/calmer and more in control during these times.

Remaining balanced and focused when facing important situations requires both a healthy physiology and strong emotional muscle. To be consciously grounded has many benefits. When you feel a sense of belonging, you will feel whole, clear-minded, and authentic. When you are in this space, this is when you will be in your zone, doing your best work and being your best self.

You'll know and *feel* that you belong where you happen to be. When grounded, you can go with the flow and bend and sway only when it suits you. You won't lose your footing or your integrity.

STRENGTH BECOMES YOU

Tony Robbins is an American author, life coach, and philanthropist. He is known for his seminars and self-help books, including *Unlimited Power* and *Awakens the Giant Within*. He has been teaching the importance of a strong physiology through exercise and daily rituals throughout his career.

Also, if you haven't seen it yet, I recommend watching Amy Cuddy's TED Talk on power posing. She speaks eloquently of the power one can feel when consciously posing for confidence-building.

Both Tony Robbins and Amy Cuddy speak of the power one experiences when one feels physically strong and embodies their own body/physiology. Every health coach will tell you the same. The strength can be felt by posing and standing like Superman/woman—hands on hips or my personal favorite: posing with your arms up in the air in a "V" shape for the universal victory pose. I'm fascinated by knowing that the victory pose is found universally. It is natural for people to raise their arms high in celebration!

I do this exercise with my clients: I have them stand tall, powerfully, with head up, shoulders back, feet under their hips, and imagining their feet growing roots into mother earth. No eye-rolling, please—on second thought, go ahead and laugh; the more fun we have, the better! This posture is a simple yet powerful exercise because it has legs (no pun intended) and works.

At first, my clients try to humor me when we do this together. However, I can see the moment when they start to feel and own their strength. In some cases, the strength that had been missing for years. They automatically stand taller and more confidently. It gets them to a "feeling" place.

Mind, body, and spiritual health are fundamental to higher-level emotional states. A clear mind, a strong body, and a sense of personal value allow for the freedom to fulfill your purpose. Good things happen for people when they feel good about themselves.

I have clients that purposely grounded themselves before meetings or speaking engagements, and they rocked it! One client did this before her executive team inspected her department, another before interviewing multiple community leaders for a project that she was creating.

I do it myself as it just feels fantastic to stretch and feel grounded and physically balanced. Another unexpected plus is that it improves my posture. Love that!

Exercise

Please, try this exercise now. Try to hold your position for two to three minutes. You may surprise yourself!

- Stand up, feet under hips, shoulders back.
- Visualize that you're growing roots that go deep into the earth.
- Know your value.
- Feel your worth.

- Feel your strength.

- How easy would it be for someone to push you right now?

- Can the wind rock you?

- Can *anything* rock you now?

As mentioned in the previous section, create a metaphor for yourself that helps you feel powerful—like the redwood tree, the beautiful mountains, or even the dominant force of the ocean. You can think of your metaphor when you are faced with any challenge so that you can stand taller, lift your head, push your shoulders back, look people in the eyes, and smile.

Changing your physiology in this way can quickly remind you of your strength, value, and worth.

You can also add a personal mantra to use with your grounding pose.

For example:

- I have value.

- I am worthy.

- I am strong.

- I've got this.

- Nothing can unsettle me now.

Afterward, you will feel and understand the benefits consciously. Over time, and with practice, it can become second nature. You can visualize yourself as balanced and calm. Adding a grounding visualization to your toolbox can help you calm yourself so that you can think more logically, even in the most intense situations.

I also recommend creating a grounding routine for the children in your life if it's appropriate. I suggest that you practice grounding with them often, like a fire drill, until it becomes second nature. You can make it fun while helping them to build a stabilizing muscle.

Here are some suggested statements for grounding with children. (Add your wonderful ideas!)

- Can you feel your feet on the ground?
- Can you wiggle your arms?
- What do you see? (Is it something interesting?)
- Can you feel your butt on the chair?
- Can you stand like a superhero? (Or yoga warrior pose)
- What do you smell? (Have a scent handy that they like)
- Do you want to hold your stress ball or stuffy? (What does it feel like?)

There is something that feels sacred about consciously owning your space with your body. It seems to validate how much we do matter and how much we do belong in this world!

Summary

Being grounded helps you to engage with life and to experience the world around you properly. You will be positively impacted when you can respond to life's challenges in a peaceful and unemotional way.

There are many ways to promote this sense of balance and being. Some suggestions include:

- Taking walks
- Meditating
- Gardening
- Practicing yoga
- Art
- Music
- Playing with children
- Cooking
- Massage
- Exercise of any kind
- Puzzles
- Reading
- Creating

The possibilities are endless. If you could do anything once you are clear and grounded, what would it be?

Chapter 4

GREMLINS

The inner voice is a powerful force;
a kind inner voice promotes an
unshakable confidence.

Introduction

Do you now feel the impact of clarity and feeling grounded? Then it's time for the next step. As invigorating as these two states are and feel—there is nothing more healing and freeing than questioning long-held negative thoughts and changing them with positive thoughts. Nothing!

A Gremlin is a fleeting negative thought that is particularly hard to grasp and extract. Ah, but when you do grasp it and extract it—well then—there is the game-changer!

Have you ever heard a catchy tune that you just cannot get out of your head? You keep hearing it, singing it, and humming it…it can be fun, right?

Your limiting thoughts began much the same way. In some cases, you have repeated them to yourself so many times that they have become your truth. You believe them because you created them and may even still bow to them.

Gremlins—those limiting thoughts—are like that catchy tune. However, they are not fun or friendly. They hinder/ bully/block you where you are the most vulnerable. It is a vicious cycle that can keep you on a hamster wheel of negativity. You continue to be vulnerable because of your self-made talk—your Gremlins.

They are insidious negative judgments by you, about you. Insidious because you are not aware of them until you become conscious of how you think. They may have kept you safe at some point in your life. Perhaps these thoughts stopped you from trying and then ultimately failing, or they reminded you about times when you did fail. They became stronger, more embedded, and much more treacherous.

Like a virus, Gremlins become systemic, until you believe them! They become your (perceived) truth, and they keep you safe, but they also keep you stuck and prevent you from believing in your most powerful self.

Can a thought be changed? Yes, it can! Can healing from our Gremlins be easy when they have had such power over us? Yes, it can! The simplified answer to a negative internal dialog is to change your dialog. Negativity brings negativity. Positivity and joy bring positivity and joy. So how are we going to get there? Questioning one negative thought at a time!

As a child, when you were yelled at, you must have deserved it, right? That's because to a child, an adult is all-knowing. When you were frowned at, you may have felt shame. How many times did you hear the word "no"? How many rules were you forced to follow? Could you question authority? Did you have a voice? What was the energy like in your home? Did you feel safe? How did you make sense of these things for yourself?

When you fail at something, you can feel as if you are a failure. The truth is that failing is only a lesson. When someone thinks someone else is pretty, some of us can become not so pretty. When some of us don't get the grades, we are stupid. When you don't make the team, you are a loser. If someone else is called skinny, you must be fat. When you don't get the position, it confirms that you just aren't worthy. And on we go, creating more powerful Gremlins (stories) to limit our progression.

Gremlins can keep you from expanding your life, the one you can have when you truly believe in yourself.

The gist is these thoughts are embedded into our psyches and can stay with us for life. They are not empowering; they are limiting. The challenging aspect is that they become real because you converted them into a truth. They come back so quickly, by rote, that you don't realize when they are activated or that you are listening to them.

Until you do!

Your Gremlins limit your growth. You will only rise in life to the level that your Gremlins allow you to. What you think absolutely has that much power over you. A Gremlin is a descriptive (and uncomfortable) name for thoughts that hinder self-esteem, actions, and progress in life. They are an internal dialog that you want to bring out of hiding so they will no longer sabotage you.

What do we know for sure?

- We are unconscious of them.
- They were created to keep us safe from harm.
- You/we turned them into a truth—which makes them harder to recognize.
- They are not conscious thoughts.
- They can harm and hinder.
- They can be changed.

As we grow and mature, we no longer need our Gremlins. If we keep them around after we should have outgrown them, they become anchors. Our goal is to recognize them and knowingly deactivate them.

Try this the next time you don't feel good about yourself. Sit quietly and ask yourself why. Why am I feeling this way? What am I trying to do, accomplish, and/or feel that brought this negative feeling upon me?

Then, just listen. When you become quiet and listen consciously to your thoughts, it can expose them.

- Is it true that I always fail at everything that I do?

- How do I want to feel?

- What do I want to believe now?

- What do I choose to believe about myself?

- Do I want to continue to beat myself up?

- What purpose are my Gremlins serving now?

- What purpose did they originally serve?

What if you realize that growth comes with mistakes and that they are normal? What if?

Didn't Thomas Edison say that "I have not failed. I've just found 10,000 ways that won't work."? That translates to 9,999 times he could have given up if he believed the steps that didn't work were failures. He chose to use those steps as an opportunity to gain knowledge, and he persevered. He was one of the most famous and prolific inventors of all time.

With conscious thinking, how can you begin to speak kindly to yourself? How can you create a conscious new tape to play?

For one thing, you can get serious about listening to your thoughts. Create a list of accomplishments that you have. If you can think of more than ten, fantastic—keep going. If you can't think of ten, ask a friend or family member for some help.

Be very honest: go down memory lane and remember what you were doing and how it felt to be motivated and accomplishing things. What have you accomplished? Who have you helped? What skills did you use? What comes easy to you? List them.

Owning your superpowers will bring self-confidence and permit you to share them with others. The "knowing" that, yes, these gifts are worthwhile and should be shared will create an alignment with your purpose.

Please read the next paragraph carefully.

Your innate strengths are inherent for a reason. You hone them almost unconsciously because they came easily to you. Because they come easy, you may not even know the level of them. If you use them strategically they can become your superpower. You may notice that you have an unusual interest in certain subjects. Be proud of what you know—these strengths make you uniquely who you are and may lead you to your life purpose!

You do not need to have an interest in and excel in everything to be a successful person. If there is an area where you are not so strong, because of a lack of interest, then let those who are interested in those areas enjoy them and share what they love; it does not make you a failure. It's just not your lane!

You learn what you can from others, and they from you. And that is more than good enough. Know that they have their gifts, and you have yours. Develop your own, and do not be envious of others' gifts. Be impressed by them—and of course, by your own.

It is healthy to take time to slow down and consciously think each day. I encourage you to take at least five minutes three times each day to take personal stock. How do I feel? Why am I feeling this way? What other perspective can I have? If you are feeling good, take note of that as well and keep it up. Consider journaling your thoughts.

Elizabeth's story

I want to introduce you to Elizabeth. She is intelligent, personable, and funny with a bright, beautiful smile. She came to coaching to work on her intense social anxiety. She was tired of making herself small because she felt shy and insecure in social situations.

Why would she hide these positive character traits from the world? Yet this happens all the time. It is a bewildering feeling for someone to have so much to offer yet not be able to dig quite deep enough to bring it out into the open. Because in the recesses of our being, and underneath all the insecurity, we know in order to be fulfilled we must find our way!

I believe that our authentic selves know that we are good enough already and that it causes us continued angst and anguish to limit ourselves. I also wholeheartedly believe this is where most life regrets stem from—not being true to yourself. In other words, not finding the way to own your good enough-ness, if you will. After Elizabeth had a conversation with anyone, she would berate herself and grade her performance. No wonder discussions were always hard work for her! As a young girl, she was sexually abused. Sadly, her parents did not believe her. This was a betrayal that deeply scarred her, leaving her feeling unprotected.

Elizabeth began to believe that she was not good, smart, or brave enough. Constantly, she reminded herself of those things, putting herself down and negatively affecting her confidence.

This incredibly caring woman talked to herself in this negative way all the time. She came to understand that her Gremlins were hindering every part of her life. She didn't deserve this kind of treatment from anyone, let alone from herself. She hadn't had the protection when she most needed it, so she created the Gremlins to keep her safe—and out of the game of her life.

With this sort of negative self-talk and constant overthinking, you can bet that there are people around all too willing to confirm these kinds of thoughts for you. Aligning ourselves with like-minded people, be it negative or positive, is common and is not done consciously. The people we associate with can help us to stay within our self-limiting comfort zone. We share our fears and Gremlins instead of our strengths and power.

I'm sure that you have heard the expression "misery likes company." Well, so does joy!

We worked first on gaining clarity and strength so that Elizabeth could come from a more secure place. Our relationship was crucial. She was skittish and terrified of her thoughts—her story was all that she had. She had to trust me and trust herself. Working with me was a huge step for her.

Elizabeth had so many Gremlins that her Gremlins seemed to have Gremlins! Each time she tried to feel more confident and proud, she would have a negative thought. She was challenged by years—almost a lifetime—of negative stories that she genuinely believed about herself.

With time and a lot of repetition, she understood the concept of how these unconscious thoughts were self-sabotaging, and she became eager to make a change.

We put together a detailed strategic plan to help foster empowerment. She had flown through the clarity process. She knew oh so well that she did not want to remain in this state. She did not want to be afraid any longer and did not want to pass her fears to her daughter. She wanted a full life! She could ground herself in the moment, but nothing was as strong as her Gremlins. She needed to take action, and she did!

I wanted to help her create a healthy perspective that she could own, which could help her question and dispel many of her Gremlins.

She feared going out in public and having conversations. Performing a task was nearly an impossibility. I wanted her to experience success both internally and externally. Due to her anxiety, I believed that it would be best to layer the steps we took to build her resilience.

The action taken needed to be strategic and impactful, engineered to move her safely out of her self-inflicted comfort zone. My goal was to help her to expand one step at a time, and then own her progress—not to become more afraid.

With her permission, I coordinated six meetings with community leaders. Each leader was chosen strategically and had something unique to offer her. They had conquered challenges themselves and had a wealth of wisdom to share. I asked Elizabeth if she would prepare a list of pertinent questions for each leader and if she would be willing to interview them. She happily agreed!

She drove herself to each meeting, met/greeted, built a rapport, and interviewed each leader. I would meet her there and keep notes for us to discuss later, not as an opportunity for her to grade herself but as a culmination of her accomplishments.

To have Elizabeth be the interviewer was a direct strategy to help her to build confidence. By nature, the interviewer's role is a proactive one, which she was not accustomed to assuming. She needed to research their positions, create a list of questions relating to their roles, drive to the meeting, and take on this leadership role. She did not miss a beat, a day—nor was she ever late for one of these meetings!

I believe that we all have leadership qualities. However, some of us pick up the mantle, and some of us do not. When given this opportunity, Elizabeth did. She became vibrant and alive. I saw nothing but wonderful possibilities for her.

Transformation happens when it becomes too painful not to change. It was distressing for her not to expand, and—with the right mix of coaxing and a team of community leaders—she did. As each meeting progressed, she became more socially comfortable. We both noticed that her questions, posture, and interview style became stronger. She walked away from each of these interviews more confident. We celebrated and acknowledged her successes!

These small successes and the positive feedback from those she interviewed had her questioning the veracity of her many Gremlins. This is key! Questioning is what a coach wants to happen. To have a client challenge their negative self-talk is pure gold! Once we are in this place, and the truth is validated—this is breakthrough-land.

Eventually, Elizabeth was asked to speak about the needs of parents and children in her community in front of an audience. Speaking in front of people was something that she would never have dared to attempt before those strategic meetings. Elizabeth found herself answering questions and comfortably offering important insights. When she told me about this meeting, she was deservedly proud. There was an incredible positive energy to her.

This work planted seeds for her future. Finding clarity gave her insight into what she wanted. Being grounded steadied her and gave her the strength she needed to question her Gremlins and to take action to move out of her comfort zone—where she came alive! This is a feeling place, and an honest one, that she will want to visit/inhabit throughout her lifetime.

As we were wrapping up her coaching sessions, she shared that she can hardly believe where she is now. She told me this as she shook her head back and forth, smiling—almost in wonder. I asked her if she could see herself accomplishing a particular dream that she always thought was out of reach. She smiled and said that she wouldn't be surprised. I just sat there and beamed inside as I knew that I was witnessing a transformation.

Reflection

When someone has been abused, and it occurred before they could understand that the abusive treatment was wrong AND NOT ABOUT THEM, they can absolutely believe that they deserved the treatment they received. They may profoundly believe that they are inferior and worthless. The truth is that we know consciously that the abuser was in the wrong. However, we need to get to the Gremlins and set them right.

Of course, wouldn't it have been nice if Elizabeth received help earlier? It could have been different if an adult had stepped in and helped her to get through it properly at the time. They might have told her, "The abuser was in the wrong. You did nothing wrong. Let me help you to heal—to listen to you and keep you safe." Yes, wouldn't that have been nice!

Abused children are forced to be adults before having the faculties to do so; abused children do whatever they can to maintain stability. They tell themselves stories about the abuse because they need to make sense of the senseless. They try to protect themselves in the only way that they know how. But they are only children and these stories are like putting a band-aid on a broken leg and continuing to walk on it.

So, enter Gremlins: I am not worthy to be believed. My voice does not matter. I am weak. I must feel shame. If I make myself unattractive, I won't be touched/hurt again. If I become small and silent, I can hide. Perhaps food, smoking, alcohol, and pills will not only numb my pain, but they also won't let me down, yell at me, hurt me, shame me.

Until, of course, they do.

Elizabeth's social anxiety was severe, and we worked through many steps and processes. I'm sharing her story in this chapter to illustrate the tremendous power that self-made Gremlins can have. Elizabeth was a slave to hers. Once she knew that—really got it—she began to break the patterns that held her down.

Her work is not done, not by a long shot, but she has a new foundation and a much stronger emotional muscle. She is a caring mother and is aware of what she is modeling for her child. Last that I heard, she was working—for one of the community leaders that she interviewed. I think that she made a good impression!

The irony is that what once kept you safe from danger, or even perceived danger, can limit your growth. Therefore, questioning your thoughts, especially when you are feeling stuck, is imperative. Sometimes, you learn to be negative/limited because it once kept you safe. It was a coping mechanism. It may have been useful at the time, perhaps even vital. An embedded coping mechanism often appears to be a truth, something that you believed couldn't be changed. Negative thoughts tend to imbed themselves deeply and stay invisible. The negative ones are the most intrusive.

Finding clarity about what you want and stabilizing yourself with grounding practices will help you differentiate between thoughts that serve you and those holding you back. You deserve this freedom.

These embedded thoughts can be unlearned simply by questioning them. When a negative thought arises, ask yourself:

- Is it true today?
- Is it helpful?
- Is it kind?
- Does it motivate me?

Can you recognize a stuck pattern in yourself? Do you think that you are self-sabotaging? Procrastinating? Fearful? Angry? Sad? If so, can you now offer yourself compassion instead?

We can mistake a pause/rest as procrastination. A more positive way to think of it is as a re-grouping. Just a gathering of our resources and a time for setting strategic goals for our new chapter. Doesn't it feel better to know that you are just re-fueling for your next adventure?

As you start to set your new course, I encourage you to acknowledge and align it with your innate strengths. Keeping the intentions for the life you want to live in mind will be crucial for goal setting.

Dream big. Keep taking steps in the direction of your goals. If you still doubt yourself, just begin anywhere. That is what my coffee cup says, and I am sticking to it. Keep moving forward until believing in yourself becomes second nature to you.

Each time there is a limiting thought that creeps in and tells you to give up, that you are not good enough, that you cannot do it—remember that it is only a thought. One that can and should be forcibly changed.

The next step is to stop everything and get clear, ground yourself, and confront it. When you recognize a Gremlin for what it is—flick that little sucker away. You don't want to sit and commiserate with negative thoughts. That is the recipe for prolonged misery.

An internal negative dialog can look like procrastination,

unworthiness, and vicious cycles, and in a worst-case scenario, it can result in an unfulfilled life. No, it is best to see Gremlins for what they are and flick them away.

Smile and celebrate your emotional strength when you recognize them. Do it every time!

Going Deeper

Fish would be the last creatures to discover water simply because they know nothing else. The water is invisible to them. They know no other reality, so there's nothing to compare it to. Water is to fish as the mind is to humans. The fish can't see the water, and we can't see our minds.

Once our thoughts are challenged, and we become conscious of creating positive more empowering thoughts, new possibilities are inevitable.

Begin by asking yourself:

- Do you forgive others for things that you cannot forgive in yourself?

- If yes, why do you have this double standard?

- Why not forgive yourself first, brush it off, and move forward?

We all have negative thoughts about ourselves from time to time. They can come on us so fast, furious, and often that most of us do not recognize them for what they are.

The negative impact they have can be dramatic.

Negative self-talk is nothing more than "horrible little monster" thoughts that run roughshod all over your self-confidence and undermine your efforts to attain your well-deserved happiness.

If you don't get them under control, you may not accomplish your goals or have the life you deserve.

> *You need to acknowledge very consciously, out loud, on paper, screaming from the rooftops— whatever it takes—that you are not your thoughts; thoughts are just thoughts. They can be changed from minute to minute and hour to hour. Why not replace them if they are negative?*

How can you recognize that your Gremlins are active? Ask yourself, "How do I feel?"

I remember my coach teaching me about these disturbing thoughts and how they stand in our way. Once I realized that they affected every aspect of my life, I made changes. I will share with you my practice for banishing those pesky Gremlins.

As we now know, we tend to believe that all the thoughts going around in our minds are facts. And, get this, we usually create the negative ones following embarrassing situations or when we have failed to accomplish a goal.

So, what kind of stories do you think we make up when

we are embarrassed, or we've failed at something? For example, do we tell ourselves: *No worries, you'll get it next time. Good effort: you should be proud of yourself.*

I don't think so! Like many of us, you most likely berated yourself. Some of us even do this viciously. Those thoughts go deep and become a part of our story, part of who we think we are.

Let's stop and think about that for a moment. We can make a thought a part of who we think we are. A mere thought! When Elizabeth understood that her negative thoughts were just stories that she was telling herself, that moment was when everything began to change for her.

> *Our worries are stories, not facts. If your Gremlins are left unchecked, you may allow these false stories to sabotage your happiness and keep you from what you are meant to accomplish! These thoughts should have as much power as a feather in the wind. Puff, they are gone.*

My heartfelt wish that you will incorporate this "remove negative self-talk" work into your empowerment goals. I am convinced that it will take years off your climb to success and happiness. Just imagine what the practice of kicking these monsters to the curb will do for you now and down the road for your children and children's children. What will they accomplish when they've always known that they are good enough?

That is a large piece of my why and purpose. And there

is not a Gremlin left that will limit me. Not now, not when I know how to send the imps away.

I've toyed with the idea of writing a book before, but I could never get beyond a few pages. Write a book? Now that was for others, not me. A Gremlin caused me to self-sabotage and kept me stuck, but eventually, with practice, it became, "Well, why not me?"

Once you work these steps, you will find that pushing through self-doubt and life's challenges will become easier. What heights can you attain by believing in yourself? And what heights will you attain if you don't?

The importance I once placed on impressing others with my wit, intelligence, and know-how all fell by the wayside! As a result, I'm compelled to tell you—and, please, hear me roar—**it is good to believe in yourself! It is healthy, and it is your right.**

We have read countless rags to riches stories, tales of incalculable failures that the most powerful and respected have endured before they have their moment in time. Are they more special than you, or is it that believing in themselves became their success factor?

I love reading about those that have overcome impossible odds. One of many incredible stories that I enjoy following is of J.K. Rowling, who overcame her Gremlins to become a universal best-selling author and one of the world's wealthiest women. A reported twelve publishing houses rejected the original Harry Potter manuscript before Rowling went from being unemployed and on welfare to becoming a multi-millionaire in five years. She wrote her initial ideas on a napkin while on a train to London.

What possesses someone to keep pushing and reaching? Where does that kind of motivation and belief come from? If the sky is the limit for some—why not you? Who did or does what you want to do? You can read their stories and perhaps mirror their success habits.

> *We can be sure that if we don't begin somewhere, strategically, we are never going to reach, let alone surpass our goals.*

You may have many Gremlins, like Elizabeth, or just a few. Everyone is different. Though, having an inner critic can be a good thing too. Think about it; it can help you to correct things about yourself that you don't like or want. The nasty ones, though, well, they have the power to bring you down hard! When you don't feel right within yourself, always remember that chances are your inner critic is working overtime.

If you have been bullied in the past, you may have internalized those circumstances, believing the cause of the bullying was all about you. In other words, you may have believed the bullies.

Bullies hurt and confuse people; they are not necessarily the best folks to consider or to even give you any feedback about who you are.

Gremlins are the most convincing untruths of all, because they come from you! You brainwashed yourself with limiting beliefs to remain safe. Whether we suffered from bullying or other difficulties in life, we are the ones that created our Gremlins! Ugh… How do you like that for a deep dive into just what lengths we will take to sabotage ourselves! However, without conscious, mature thought, we believe them to be the truth. Please re-think them now consciously, actively, and with some force.

Your thoughts are not "true;" they are just thoughts that you are having. Practice letting the negative versions flit by. Watch them go and keep on reaching for a better and more positive feeling thought. At first, I found this difficult to understand, let alone do. Now it makes perfect sense to me. With practice, it will work for you too.

You are not your thoughts. They are just explanations that you tell yourself to understand what is going on around you. You created them to make sense of things.

You can change your thoughts anytime that you choose. For instance, if you have an idea like: "I'm a loser; I am never going to learn how to do this," you can change your perspective to: "I can do this; I just need to dig in, remember my strengths, and make it happen. I've done ABC before, and I can do this now. I've got this!"

Beware of your inner dialog because it can limit every area of your life. How encouraging is it to know that you can change it? Like the bullies of the world—those hurt and scared people—how freeing is it to know that other people's negative thoughts and actions toward you are solely about them? Never you!

That was true when you were two years old, and it is still true today. The more crazed, dysfunctional, and challenged the childhood, perhaps the easier it is for you to trigger back to your Gremlins. Consider the unfathomable amount of time we play back an inaccurate and biased account of our failures instead of our accomplishments!

There is a cause and effect to our thoughts. When we do one thing another will happen. They create an energy that we feel physically. We can change this energy by changing our words, stories, and thoughts. Isn't it freeing to know this? It took me a while to recognize my negative self-talk for what it was. Once I could, I just kept sending those Gremlins on their merry way! I laugh now at some of the thoughts that used to have power over me.

Sometimes, I will make a flicking motion with my hand to send the little Gremlin away. That gesture alone makes me smile. It is an action that validates my positive inner dialog. It helps to empower me further. You can do this too!

Before, if I wanted to do something bigger and better, to grow, expand, and uplift my life in some way, I would think, "Who do you think you are? Really, who?" And does that mean that I ultimately became my own bully?

I'm hoping the next time you don't feel good about yourself and don't know why, you will consider a Gremlin at play. From now on, when you have those moments, try to catch yourself to discover:

- What are you thinking?
- How can you change that thought to a more positive and productive one?

It takes practice to begin recognizing unconscious thoughts for what they are. You can do this, and you must do this!

Exercise

Suppose you can consciously accept that your Gremlins came to you unconsciously. In that case, you know that you have automatically/robotically written a story about yourself that isn't based on the truth and has hindered you.

If you do accept that you can change your thoughts, then you can consciously create a new story. Isn't a conscious story apt to be more truthful anyway?

If you answered yes—then write a new story. Seriously, write at least a paragraph about your positive traits and strengths before moving on to the next step. Picture yourself clear, worthy, and in control of your Gremlins. Think about it as a new beginning.

Summary

If you don't feel good about yourself, suspect a Gremlin. It is an ugly monster that sits on your shoulder, whispering untruths in your ear, like...

I am:

- a failure
- a loser
- ugly
- fat
- a fraud
- stupid
- mean
- old
- stuck
- lost
- unlovable

Or a Gremlin can remind you of all the things you're not:

I'm not:

- smart
- educated
- strong

- young
- old
- big
- fit
- thin
- religious
- good-looking
- born into it
- rich

When you know better, this will become the nonsense to you that it truly is!

Understanding where the Gremlins come from and how they developed can help us to defeat them.

If you only have one takeaway from reading this book, I genuinely want you to understand deep down that you already are good enough. You can dream big. Please, go ahead and dream your biggest dreams. The bigger, the better because you can attain it if you are committed and can visualize it. Your psyche will not let you dream outside the realm of your possibilities. So, go for it!

I believe this so strongly now that I allow my dreams to be bigger than ever. I know that they can be realized. As I write this to you, I know that I will publish this book. My readers will either like it or not. Either way, I will not feel diminished. I will do my best, and that is all that any of us can do.

It is simple, really. My, how simple things can be when we let go of our emotional blocks! I hope that you will come to embody this empowering and healing truth.

I'll meet you in the next chapter when you are ready to move on.

Chapter 5

NEGATIVE AND POSITIVE ENERGY

Introduction

Energy is everywhere. It can be both positive and negative. Your energy extends like water into every corner of your life. Remember the ripple effect from tossing the stone into the pond at the beginning of this book?

Energy is contagious, and it gets passed on from one person to another. The truth is energy can take many forms. If your perspectives of life are more fear-driven and you view the world from a negative standpoint, you can't help but radiate negative energy. Your unconscious thoughts and beliefs can turn you into a negative person without being aware of it. One more reason to deal with those pesky Gremlins! Just as your positive thoughts and actions turn you into a positive, more vibrant, and all-around happier person!

If negativity is so ingrained that you don't notice it, how

do you stop attracting the wrong people, the wrong situations, and the wrong feelings? How can you be sure you're not unconsciously perpetuating that negativity? When you intentionally deal with your negative inner dialog, you can become aware and conscious of what you are thinking, doing, and emitting. Question your thoughts, how you're feeling – how are you showing up?

> *The good news is that negative energy can be transformed.*

Why transform it? For happiness's sake. Negative energy robs you of joy and wellbeing, while positive energy invigorates and keeps you in a state of joy, happiness, and good health.

Our thoughts have energy which can be either negative or positive.

An ad for an employment opportunity caught my eye recently. A yoga studio in my area was looking for "positive" people to apply for a front desk receptionist position. Skills are important, but attitude and how people show up can be even more so.

The way that you show up in life matters, and not just a little. Your family, friends, colleagues, and everyone around you are affected by your energy, actions, and mindset. Plus, you are affected by theirs as well. Although in truth, the more you are aware of energy drains and energy gifts, the more you will be able to recognize when negative or positive energy is present.

When brain scientist Dr. Jill Bolte Taylor was recovering from a stroke, she shared in her excellent TED Talk that her visitors must be responsible for the energy that they brought into her hospital room.

Why did she need her guests to be responsible for their energy? It's because positive energy is healing, and negative energy is draining. While she was vulnerable and recuperating from her stroke, she could not risk her health. She knew instinctively that she was not strong enough, in her vulnerable state, to protect herself from negative energy.

We all can grasp what she means. Even though energy is an unseen force, much like a puff of wind, we sure can feel it. All of us have been in the presence of both positive and not-so-positive energy. We have walked into a room and felt the tension in the air. It is safe to say that one's negative energy comprises many Gremlins. Unlike the internal negative talk, the energy we disperse is felt by others.

Your energy and mood are contagious!

I once met someone who was in such a positive mood that it was impossible to remain grouchy around her. As she grabbed our hands and we danced in a circle in the middle of a sports field, all of us in the group ended up laughing and enjoying ourselves. Her positivity rubbed off onto us.

In contrast, I've been around the type of person who will kill any pleasant mood. Their negative energy can suck up every ounce of pleasure from the room and puts everyone else in a bad mood too.

I love how children have a natural exuberance and quest for learning and growth. Their curiosity for life emits a pure and powerful energy that is undeniable. Could this be because they are mostly (hopefully) Gremlin free?

Similarly, you know if your spouse, boss, siblings, parents, children, teachers, students are happy, sad, angry, disappointed, or feeling at peace just by the energy that they emit.

Haven't we all had these experiences of feeling and sensing energy? And can this knowledge help us?

Love and Fear: The Energy Carriers

There are two extremes of emotions: love and fear. Are your emotions primarily residing with the lower-lever feelings closer to fear, such as hate, frustration, depression, sadness, anger, and jealousy, or are they with the higher-level feelings closer to love, joy, enthusiasm, compassion, passion, confidence, self-love, positivity, etc.? Where do you want your emotions to be? What will you bring to others and manifest for yourself if you stay in those lower-level feelings? What will you bring to others and create for yourself when you feel the higher levels of emotion?

Remember that we can pass on our mood/energy to those around us. What sort of mood do you want to pass on? How do you want people to feel around you?

As important as your energy is for all aspects of your life, it is imperative when you're dealing with children. I always come back to the child because 1) you were once a child, and that is where many of your thoughts were born, which gives you a great starting place for resolution, and 2) because children are so very vulnerable to our energy. How their adults unconsciously or consciously show up may inflate or deflate them.

As an adult, if you are around an angry person who is raging and spouting off, you will most likely hightail it out of there. But sadly, a child cannot leave if this kind of energy is in the home. They are stuck there to absorb all of it because there is no other option. Children are like sponges, open and constantly learning. How people show up with their children is by far more important to the child's development than any STEM program or scholastic achievement will ever be.

Reflection

Food for thought: not feeling safe for extended periods or too often, changes who a child is and who they become. We already have our built-in Fight or Flight reflex; we don't need to absorb everyone else's! Yet, generationally, this is something that happens. We need to wake up and be conscious of what was done to us and is something we could be doing to others.

Suppose you have experienced this negativity in your life. In that case, you'll want to recognize it, do your work, and ensure you do not continue to suffer the consequences or, even worse, start to pass the behavior on to the next generation. You need to focus on much higher-level thoughts and future actions.

If you discover there is something that you are already doing to others, you can and should stop it. With awareness and understanding of the ramifications that this type of behavior can cause, there's an excellent chance you will succeed in stopping. If you're reading this book, that's a good sign that you're ready to change.

If you are ready to accept responsibility for your actions, then breathe and know that children can heal from all kinds of dysfunction. You can ask for their forgiveness and make a massive effort to turn things around.

For it to work, it will have to be not only for today but from now on. It is the only way that that they will trust you again. Their healing will not happen UNTIL they can believe and trust in the new and HEALED you. Take some parenting classes or work with a professional so you can save them from a litany of issues and end the repeating cycle.

When it seems that you are attracting negativity from people, the chances are quite good that you were at one time emitting some negative energy. Look inside and be honest about what you are bringing to the situation. What do you need to change? What can you change?

Have you inherited other people's ways of thinking? Perhaps you have absorbed your parents'/friends'/colleagues' or even society's way of thinking. Ask yourself what brought about these supposed truths for these people.

If you look at the history of what was once culturally accepted by the collective—about religion, gender, sex, race, politics, the environment, and more—you cannot help but acknowledge that the world continues to evolve and that it is our collective duty to grow with it.

None of us is perfect and understanding positive energy is not about that anyway. It is about feeling better and being your best self! Difficulties and challenges are a part of life. People will lose jobs, become disabled, get sick, and they will die. Loss of all kinds will occur as the world is every changing. Real heartbreak will come to all of us. Life will go on. What we have inside of us is a powerful instinct to live on as well—contribution and love are great energy healers.

Going Deeper

Remember that knowing what you do not want is valuable knowledge. I don't want to bring negativity to others. I don't want others to inflict their negative energy on me! Conversely, I want to be a source of comfort, happiness, and peace to those I love.

> *Act powerfully! You need to draw a line in the sand and live your life like yesterday was yesterday, and today is today—and you thankfully (if needed) have outgrown yesterday.*

Start by feeling the energy your thoughts hold. There comes a time in every coaching session when I ask a client if something feels right. Does it resonate with you? How does it feel in your belly/core? In these moments, I have never once had a client that doesn't understand those questions. Getting quiet and listening to yourself can help you to develop your philosophy for life.

Have you ever asked yourself what your philosophy of life is?

Our families/guardians didn't mean to stifle our growth. They felt they had views and experiences to share with us. For the most part, they wanted to protect us. In some cases, they did it through religion, prejudice, keeping our world small, discipline/rigidity, narrow thinking, etc.

Of course, not everything was negative; many of those experiences handed down were beneficial as well.

With the helicopter view that you now have as an adult, it can be interesting to look back and remember which situations empowered you or deflated you in your young life. What do you still carry with you today? What do you need to release? How do you want to share moving forward in life?

How can you heal from this "acquired" negative energy and transform yourself into the new, more positive you? There is no quick fix; it will take as long as it takes.

For those that inherited a lot of negativities, know that you never deserved any of it. If you were harmed or diminished, I am sorry for that. Please know that it was never about you. It is always about someone else's lack of character, clarity, knowledge, etc.

There is also no quick fix for the perpetrators of your pain who now want to be forgiven. As we advance, their actions must speak louder than their words. Those who harmed you must take responsibility for past actions, moving forward with honesty and compassion. Then, over time, when their positive behavior is stronger and more constant than their past negative behavior, trust can set in, and perhaps your forgiveness will be the result. Depending on the harm done, however, it may take years for you to trust them again truly.

Depending on the situation, sometimes you must cut your losses. Staying in a damaging relationship isn't healthy. It feeds negativity and can diminish every aspect of your life.

Luckily, our energy can be healthier in short order with some new habits and understandings.

We know that there are many unhappy and confused millionaires and billionaires. Therefore, we know that money cannot buy us love, happiness, or even remarkable energy. An irony of energy is that we credit animals with reading people's energy but have not considered how we humans read and feel each other's energy.

Researchers have long known that negative emotions program our brains for a specific action. When danger or perceived danger crosses our path, we freeze, run, or fight. The rest of the world doesn't matter at that moment. We are focused entirely on the fear we feel.

In other words, the fight-or-flight reflex narrows our perception to the point of solely focusing on survival. It is a valuable instinct if one must go into survival mode because the danger is physically tangible. The problem is that our brains are also programmed to respond to intangible negative emotions with the same fight-or-flight response. We strike out in anger or run away when perhaps a smile, joke, kind word, or conversation could solve an issue far more effectively.

If you bring negativity to a situation, you invite it right back into your life. It will keep coming until you learn what you need to learn. Just imagine what can happen with your relationships and life if your first impulse is to smile and respond with kindness—not just for a day or a week but until that becomes your norm.

Until you decide to make this change, there will never be real forgiveness or trust either from you or others.

I recently read an interesting review of a self-help book. The reviewer stated that usually, these books could motivate you for a week or two, and then you're right back to do the same old thing. That reviewer's words hit home.

Like all other "self-helpers," I'd like to believe that real and lasting change can happen from insight and the "aha" moments. I also think that timing, preparation, and a powerful desire for lasting change must be present in the first place. For me, a decision to change must include:

- An unequivocal commitment.
- A line drawn in the sand, never to be crossed again.
- A desire created by enough confusion and pain to catapult you in a new direction.

At some point in life, we make our luck. The difference between the lucky and unlucky people is that lucky people do their work—hence they are prepared for their opportunities. They become confident, ready, and believe in themselves.

Yet even when you practice positivity and do your work, you can certainly still be triggered back to your old way of thinking, and you occasionally will be. You have been unconsciously attuned to old negative thoughts and programming repeatedly until you believed it all! Now that you are conscious of these patterns and your emotional strength continues to expand, you will not stay in that place for any length of time. You will more quickly recognize that those thoughts are Gremlins and push them away.

Self-care partnered with positive thoughts can go a long way towards helping us to shift out of a negative state. We must all strive to uplift our thoughts, to uplift our lives. *Isn't that growth?* Energy and action will follow, our environments will be healthier, and those we interact with will feel uplifted and positive.

Striving to do this—not just for today, but as a way forward—will make families stronger and happier, resulting in added successes for everyone, and perhaps a more positive standard of living will continue to emerge.

Both positive and negative energy are contagious. Take the time to consider this fact. Ask yourself which energy you want to feed. Because it is true what you take in is what you will emit. Positive energy can bring happiness, health, and success to you and those around you. Negative energy produces the opposite.

Can you coach yourself to a new, more comfortable you? Yes, you can! Can you surround yourself with positive people, read self-help books, and have "aha" moments? Of course you can! Can you hire a coach, find a mentor, or look for role models? You can, and you are because you're reading this book!

So, if you believe that you can make that shift to positivity, why wait? Be diligent in this because you are truly meant to be happy, confident, and free to live a creative life. Keep yourself as positive as possible; always reach for a better feeling. When you feel better about yourself, it will emanate from every area of your life.

Exercise

Write down your answers to these questions, then reflect on those answers. What are you doing right? How can you do better?

- Who do you love?
- How does your energy show up for them?
- How do you WANT to show up?
- How does your energy resonate with others?
- How do you WANT it to resonate with others?

Try these quick three-minute tips for changing your energy:

- Dance—change your physiology, move thy body!
- Sing
- Laugh

Use these suggestions to create a lasting shift to positive energy:

- Cultivate self-love.
- Push negative thoughts away.
- Don't gossip.
- Do what you love!
- Share laughter with someone daily.
- Take care of your health.
- Practice gratitude.
- Give to others.

Summary

Research shows that by being a positive person, we make ourselves and others happier and healthier. That's a lot of responsibility! We need to be aware of the type of energy we are exuding and its effect on our surroundings. We also need to be aware of the impact that the energy of others has on us or has had on us while we were growing up.

- How will you create a healthy, positive life?
- Are you willing to release the old pattern that is causing negative reactions?
- Can you commit to taking your power back by releasing negativity?

By recognizing how negative energy starts and where it comes from, we can turn the negative into positive.

Chapter 6

PERFECTIONISM AND OTHER
BLOCKS

Introduction

Perfection is a myth. It is a myth of astronomical proportions. A desire for perfection left unchecked will limit your growth and, most certainly, your happiness.

Can a person be happy chasing the unattainable?

Can a project ever be complete?

Are you deluding yourself if you think that you can or even *should* be perfect?

If we get to a clear-thinking place—and can reverse-engineer every project known to man from the invention of the wheel to solar power—can we agree that these inventions, already amazing when launched, continue to evolve even today? The wheel originated from a seed of an idea and became a reality, evolving its uses over thousands of years. Many ideas have many contributors adding their ingenuity to various creations/inventions. Is an invention ever complete? Is there always room for improvement?

> *If we want to get down to the basics about it, there is always room for growth.*

So, what is the problem with perfectionism? Firstly, perfectionism links to fears of insecurity and inadequacy, which contribute to depression, anxiety, or even more severe health problems like eating disorders or mortality. Thus, perfectionism can be stressful and, if left unaddressed, could mean you're digging yourself into an early grave.

Not only is the "quest" for perfection harmful to your joy, but it is also painful because it can cause so much self-judgment and fear. You may have developed these perfectionistic tendencies to protect yourself from feeling inadequate and getting hurt. While this may have worked for you in the past, it isn't compatible with an empowered and happy life.

Trying to attain these standards is like attempting to live your life in a fairytale. It is more of an "other-worldly" goal, something a mere mortal cannot attain. In other words, perfection is just a figment of our imaginations! A lie! Therefore, if true perfection is a myth, yet you refuse to accept any standard short of it, where does that leave you?

If life is a lesson and we continue to grow and learn, how can we be perfect at any age? We can be good, great, fabulous—but, seriously, perfect? Is perfection in the eye of the beholder?

We are all unique with our perspectives. Take Pablo Ruiz Picasso, for instance. He was a Spanish painter, sculptor, poet, and playwright and is regarded as one of the most influential artists of the twentieth century.

When I view some of his artwork, I'm left wondering why. I look at his geometric pieces upside-down, sideways, and right-side-up, seeing shapes, bright colors, and facial features in places I do not expect. However, another person viewing the same work sees a masterpiece. Some would even claim perfection. I find Picasso's geometric art very interesting, and yet for others, this work is genius.

Imagine if Picasso limited his artistry to please others or chased their idea of perfection. Would he have even painted in the first place? Could perfection be just a perspective, a slightly different angle of how something is viewed?

My heart breaks for those who chase perfection, my younger self included. I remember when I could have celebrated a well-done result but was relentless in the pursuit of my standards of perfection. I had all the fears: fear of failure, fear of making mistakes, fear of disapproval, and imposter syndrome.

As mentioned previously, there are two core emotions: love and fear. If love holds the higher emotions, then it stands that fear has all the lower-level feelings. Imagine the amount of talented and gifted people who fear coming into their own, expressing themselves, and fulfilling their purpose. An untold number of amazing people have "chosen" to live a minimal life because of fear. If our younger vulnerable selves defined fear as a tsunami, can our mature adult selves now view it as just a wave—then a ripple? Can we change our perspective and see fear as a challenge or something exciting to do?

Let's tackle the falsehoods that fear would have us believe and see what resonates. If you are not hurting anyone and delivering your very best, should you even care what others think? If you do, and they decide that you or your efforts aren't good enough—what then?

Could their judgment cause you to spiral down into lower-level feelings about yourself? This could trigger your Gremlins, which can come quickly, unconsciously, and by habit to *validate* your belief that something in you is not good enough.

Now, what if you were grounded and clear about who you are?

What if without this fear you:

- Find a cure for a disease?
- Create your masterpiece?
- Invent the next great piece of technology?

- Write an amazing novel?

- Become a leader of great integrity?

- Find and share your innate talents for the good of humanity?

Would it be fair to yourself—or the world—to allow fear to keep your light from shining?

Rebecca's story

Rebecca came to coaching because she felt stuck in her career. She wasn't making any progress or moving forward in any way.

She was photograph-ready and meticulously dressed every time we met. It was evident that she took great pride in doing everything perfectly.

I learned that Rebecca had grown up in a strict, religious family where she and her siblings had been judged harshly. This resulted in a very high-achieving household. They believed that there was nothing more important than representing the family well. They were honor-bound to keep their dirty laundry, failures, and any dysfunctions from public view.

This begs several questions. Can high achievement be derived from a more open, giving, and comfortable environment? Can we be raised/live in a home that promotes confidence and achievement yet still offers a soft place to land? Of course!

The point here is that a perfect façade (think smoke and mirrors) can be created from fear. In Rebecca's case, she was left with her childhood armor still on and without a sense of her natural entitlement for freedom of purpose and happiness. There were Gremlins in the closet!

Rebecca's siblings not only worked hard to keep up appearances to not tarnish the family name, but they also punished those who failed. I understood her well because I had been raised in a similar environment. We talked a lot about always needing to be right (which just makes others wrong). We all know how that feels! Since she was always attempting to do what was right, Rebecca didn't understand why she didn't see her expected winning results.

I shared a lesson with Rebecca that I will share with you here. I asked her if she knew of someone or had a friend that was, perhaps, a bit of a "hot mess." Maybe that person was loud, drank too much alcohol, talked too much, laughed too loud, hugged everyone constantly— you get the picture. (Now, I'm not advocating doing anything too much, mind you!)

And then I asked her, "Have you ever noticed just how much everyone likes that person?"

Well, I honestly thought that I had lost her because she turned and stared out of the window for ages. After what seemed like forever to me, she turned with such a sincere look on her face and whispered, "Yes."

She seemed stunned. She did have a friend that

immediately came to mind and asked me, "Why is that?" She went on to share this person's failings and gifts. She saw how everyone flocked to be this person's friend, leaving Rebecca feeling left out and confused.

We considered the potential reasons why this friend was so attractive to others.

- Are people more relaxed around her?
- Could her energy be lighter, more fun?
- Perhaps she doesn't expect anything from others, and people can just be themselves in her company.

We stayed in this space for a long time because this had made such a monumental impact on her. I appreciated that a significant change in thinking had taken place. Rebecca realized that this wall of perfectionism she'd kept up for most of her life—to keep her safe from ridicule in a competitive and demanding family—was no longer needed. Maybe it was never really needed at all.

As a result, she reframed her ideas about perfection, resolving to try her best. She realized that being right all the time is not only stressful, but it can be off-putting to others. Who wants to constantly be made wrong, never to be allowed to win?

This realization gave Rebecca permission to be more vulnerable, to lighten up on herself and to feel comfortable showing off her goofball side publicly.

In this more relaxed state, she was able to bring more fun energy home to her family and her work. She soon moved forward with some *creative* business ideas and found her voice at work in the process.

Perfectionism out; creative energy in!

I am thrilled to have been Rebecca's coach. She is an intelligent and honorable woman. She has children that she adores and wants to raise knowing they are always good enough and they don't have to jump through hoops to earn that place.

She is creating an environment that is a safe place to land. One that is filled with peace, encouragement, and possibilities.

An aside here:

For some, it may be difficult to grasp or believe that you have special skills, talents, and greatness in you. It may feel arrogant or even a little narcissistic. In truth, it can sometimes be challenging to distinguish confidence from arrogance—or worse.

I recently had a deep conversation with a wonderful teacher/coach/author friend who struggled with whether she was "good enough." This woman is religious, studies Kabbala, and is currently ghostwriting a book on Judaism with a rabbi friend. Intellectually, she does know that she is good enough and that everyone else is as well. But intellect is not emotions.

On this day, however, she needed absolute proof. She

needed to know this in every fiber of her being so that she could be soothed by the feeling of it and could keep moving forward.

I asked her to think of the most significant person in the universe. Who did she respect above all others? Who is the brightest, most famous person of all time to her? I felt that she needed to hold this person in the highest of esteem.

She dug deep and finally chose someone. I then asked her to hold out her right hand and to picture this esteemed person as a newborn baby, placed in her right hand and presented to the world as the gift that they are. She sat in front of me with her right hand outstretched.

"Now hold out your left hand and place your newborn self in that hand," I instructed. "A tiny you—a newborn baby offered as a gift to the world." She sat there before me, holding out both of her hands, looking at me with her earnest and kind face.

I then asked her to please tell me which baby God preferred.

Let that marinate.

She laughed, she cried, and most importantly, she understood—to her core—a truth that she always wanted to believe.

I know, right? How can it be that you are as much a gift to the world as all others? How can it not be? Each person is born important to the world, special, good enough already, and we always will be. We are the cake! The rest is just the frosting. It comes down to how we think about ourselves and what we do or don't do with those thoughts.

It is not arrogant or narcissistic to know that you are good enough already and always have been. It is harmful to you not to know it. With narcissism, there is a lack of empathy towards others and a sense of entitlement over others. That is not you. So, you can take that right out of the equation!

Reflection

Perfectionists can carry criticism of both themselves and others. It is a heavy burden to bear and a debilitating one at that. By setting standards at unachievable levels, i.e., perfection, we set ourselves up for failure.

There is nothing wrong with setting high standards. We should all strive to be the best we can be, but the standard we set for ourselves must be within reach. It's all about being human and doing our best.

Ironically, letting go of perfectionism allows for much greater accomplishments—because we are not afraid to try!

If perfectionism is an issue for you, please don't skip this work!

Perfectionism is just one of the falsehoods that can hold

us back. Here are some others, which may all be linked with perfectionism.

Fear of being judged

If the judgment you fear is coming from another's opinion and thoughts, does that make it true? Or is it just their perspective? Why would you make their opinion your business?

Perhaps you don't want to be found lacking in any way. You may fear others' judgment because if they judge you negatively, you will feel bad about yourself. Their opinion may even validate your lower-level negative thoughts about yourself.

Once you confront and expose an untruth, as many times as it takes, it becomes the beginning of freedom.

Should you give your power away because your Gremlins are giving you negative thoughts?

Fear of being found a fraud

Imposter syndrome is a universal fear. You may tell yourself:

- "Who do you think you are?"
- "You'll be 'found out.'"
- "The other shoe will drop."
- "You are nothing more than smoke and mirrors!"

Isn't fraud an act of deliberation? Are you purposely trying to deceive others? Doubtful!

The definition of fraud is a person or thing intended to deceive others, typically by unjustifiably claiming or being credited with accomplishments or qualities.

Assuming that you are not intentionally deceptive to others, then you are all the *professionalism, skills, strengths, and life experience* that you bring to this moment or any moment.

Are your fears and doubts a result of your inability to guarantee perfectionism? No one can; what you can do is your best, and that is truly good enough.

Can it be that you think you are a fraud because you judge yourself too harshly? Ask yourself this: *If you can't make a mistake, can you grow?*

What is the truth? Perhaps your Gremlin stories have become all too real in your mind. You must question these stories each time that you find one limiting you! Once you expose the truth, ceremoniously flick that Gremlin to where the sun doesn't shine!

> *You are good enough already, and you don't need to be perfect. Let these words sink in now and save yourself years of doubt and heartache. Don't allow these Gremlins any more time to grow even stronger.*

Fear of not being good enough

This falsehood is downright insidious, damaging, and limiting. After reading this far, perhaps you are now aware of a pattern of self-neglect and negative stories you have been telling yourself. Perhaps you are now consciously hearing that negative self-talk: not good enough, imperfect, I am a fraud, etc. This awareness is a good thing.

You are beginning to believe that these are only thoughts and beliefs activated upon insecurity, which stops your forward movement so you cannot possibly fail.

From this day forward, when you don't feel as though you are good enough, you have the tools to ground yourself and get clarity on it. Remember, clarity is your truth. It is the key to empowerment and transformation! Once you gain clarity and grasp the danger that negative self-talk presents to your happiness, accomplishments, and wellbeing, then you can consciously flick those Gremlins away.

Feeling bad sometimes is just part of being a person. Relationships get rocky, your foot won't stop itching, you're sleep-deprived, or the weather is dreary. The key is understanding that something could be up if you feel bad about yourself for no reason. Could it be an old story that is triggering you?

What if your greatness is knocking on the door? What if it is that close? Are you able to feel it pulling at you? Is it time to put away the old childish stories and fears and take hold of your life?

If life asks more of you, it's your job to answer—not to let your Gremlins squash the opportunity! Once you understand this, you'll never again think that being good enough is only for the magical few. You are magical too. You have all the gifts you need to be successful and feel empowered.

You have always been good enough!

Envy of others

We can feel bad when we covet what others have but feeling envious is nothing more than a window into what you want. It can be reframed to be informational, so you're aware of what you specifically desire: position, charisma, car, physique, money, talents, house, hair, body.

When you feel envy come over you, congratulate/bless that person, and know that you can have what you want too. You can push the feeling of envy far away and see that it is merely calling you to a higher standard for yourself. You can achieve something, or you would not have this feeling pulling at you in the first place.

From now on, when envy comes over you, smile and be grateful for that new and compelling knowledge/insight into what you do want.

Going Deeper

Whose judgment of YOU matters?

If not yours *(yet),* then learn why. Do you want to impress others, have them like you, prove your intelligence, be accepted, finally feel good enough? What is it for you?

Okay, here is the crux of the matter. If someone's judgments are made up of the many layers of who they are (including their Gremlins), then should you give your power away because of a mere thought that someone else has about you?

Let's take another angle. Are thoughts, Gremlins, and negative self-talk real? And if so, can they be limiting? I sincerely hope that you have answered with a resounding YES.

Indeed, thoughts *are* real. They do have enormous power. They do not have to be true or false; they are just thoughts—tools to help you make sense of things.

You need to break free from the lower-level thoughts you may still have of yourself. They are not compatible with your growth and the life that you want.

Exercise

Identifying the blocks holding us back is important in enabling us to clear them and move forward. Here are some ways to continue that process.

Find a quiet space. Get physically grounded and tell yourself:

- I am intelligent.
- I clean up well.
- I am a creative person.
- I have integrity.
- I have compassion.
- I am the real deal.

Smile and breathe this in. Enjoy a little self-love, friend!

Ponder these questions. Write down your answers if it helps bring more clarity.

- Has perfectionism hindered you?
- Have you worried that others would consider you inadequate?
- How will your life be better if you find peace by doing your best and not worrying if you don't achieve perfection?
- What change(s) can you make starting today that will have you thanking yourself when you are eighty-five years old?
- Write perfectionism a thank-you note for helping you to get to where you are right now. And then, in your own words, explain that your adult self can take you the rest of the way. Celebrate!

- Create a mantra.

A mantra is an affirmation to inspire you to be your best self. Its purpose is to provide motivation and encouragement for focusing your mind to achieve a goal. Mantras have been utilized around the world for thousands of years.

Create some mantras that resonate with you. For example:

- Perfection is in the eye of the beholder.
- A figment of my imagination will no longer hinder me.
- What others think is about them—not me.
- I am perfectly me.

As these statements become true for you, remember that you cannot un-know a truth once you know it!

Summary

There is an alternative to striving for perfection: aim for as good as you can be right now. Understand that everyone makes mistakes, but mistakes give us the gift of knowledge! Ironically, striving for perfection in all things can hinder us.

Do you want to reach your lofty goals? Well then, make the mistakes necessary, make lots of them, as they will become the pathway to your accomplishments. Accept your limitations and move on. Practice self-love and maintain your self-worth by being kind to yourself and others.

Everyone has doubts over their abilities from time to time, but we usually hide these doubts from others. Don't make the mistake of comparing your internal struggles with the finished product that others present to you. Everyone is a work in progress, whether you can see it or not.

It's like the old tale of a duck swimming. It looks calm and serene on the top, but it's working like crazy out of sight to get where it's going, and so are we all.

Chapter 7

EXPRESSING SELF

Introduction

We can express ourselves through art, dance, work, the environment that we create, the cultures with which we choose to surround ourselves, and by using our voice. Finding one's voice goes well beyond people talking or singing. Our voice is an expression of our thoughts, actions, and all we hold dear. Expressing yourself is one way that you can show up in life.

Being your true authentic self without fear of what others may think or say will open the floodgates to your best life. Discovering your voice is about finding your true essence once again. When a confident four-year-old child walks into a room, you see that their shoulders are back, their head is held high, their stride is confident, and a smile is at the ready. They march forward, oblivious to people's judgments. In the best case, a child's essence is one of knowing that they belong.

I believe there is always a part of all of us that knows that we are whole. That part starts showing up again as we become more mindful. If you are on a search for wholeness and authenticity, you are already on the path there. Perhaps it's buried a bit, but it can shine bright again with a little work, self-understanding, and love.

I know of parents who saddle their children with every ounce of dissatisfaction that they have experienced. In the short run, they may gain an ally—and perhaps even a child that will end up taking care of them—but this is never good! How can it be good? The parent should be the parent.

Then when their children regurgitate all this pent-up frustration into society and their own families, everyone is left wondering what is wrong with *the child*!

There seems to be a parenting revolution happening. An evolution where it is the rule to be mindful and raise children with the concept that they are just that: children! They're not cohorts who exist to absorb an adult's feelings and challenges. We have six human needs; when all are met, we feel whole. More on these needs in Chapter 10.

The power of our parents' reach can be felt for a lifetime! Their collected stories, grief, anger, lack of many things can be carried by us. Add the collected stories of our spouse, our colleagues, society—and the burden can become overwhelming. Where should it end, and with whom?

We've covered much of what caused so many of us to feel unsure of ourselves already. I am only focusing on creating an understanding of the negative to show that there is a healthier way. We *can* also receive and carry forth confidence, positivity, and belief, adding to it as needed.

Listen to your inner voice that says you are good enough. Good enough for just about anything that tickles your fancy. In all seriousness, you are! If you don't find your way, you can bet that someone else will find it for you.

If you have something to learn, say, and do, I hope that you will find the courage to express it. Hiding behind a wall of quiet is self-limiting as well as self-punishing. If you are coming from a place of clarity and being grounded, chances are you will not go wrong.

Not listening to the internal dialog of your true worth, not finding your voice and living your truth, is denying who you are. You'll never stop pining for your essence, so allow yourself to step up and be you—sooner!

Your speaking voice is also a unique signature of who you are. It has a timbre like no other; it can depict happiness, seriousness, anger, calm, intensity, love, and more. It carries your thoughts to your listeners. Your voice can add value; it can calm a situation or bring levity to it. Also, it can transmit your energy, help to calm a frightened child or animal.

Now, if only texting and emails could depict our voice accurately. Hence, the emoji to soften the written word.

My story

I've always been impressed by accomplished public speakers. For most of my life, I feared public speaking. In front of people, I would become an I-want-to-hide, voiceless version of myself. I teetered between freezing and fleeing. I was afraid of being judged.

I am in the business of growth and transformation, so I needed to ask myself point-blank and with no fluff where my Gremlins/stage fright came from. For me, my fear was "stage" related, more about standing alone with several people listening and looking.

I wonder if it could have had its beginning back to the third grade when I was chosen as one of two leads in my school's play. During tryouts, on stage among my peers, I was loud enough and expressive enough to convince the music teacher that I could do the role of Mother Rabbit proud.

During rehearsals, I continued to grow into the role, my costume added to my sense of confidence, and the stage was set. This was all good stuff!

On opening day, when the curtain ceremoniously crept slowly open, I, Mrs. Rabbit, completely froze. To this day, I can still see the expression on the poor music teacher's face. And even at the young age of nine years old, I made up a story: "I bet she wishes that she never chose me. I let her down. The other lead was the real deal. I always let people down!" (Gremlins born.)

I could have focused on being chosen as one of the two

leads to be "Mother Rabbit," but nope, like so darn many of us, I focused on my failure and the negative—my freezing.

Have you ever had one of those moments when time seems to stand still, and you wanted nothing more than to escape? How old were you? We have all had a moment like this. How wonderful it would be if we were raised to focus and celebrate all the good! Not in an arrogant way, but to highlight and understand a strength. How validating it would be to be told to view challenges and bumps in the road as a necessary learning curve.

I'd like to tell you that was the first and last time that I couldn't push through my fear, but that just wouldn't be true. For many years, I allowed my Gremlins to control my growth. I validated the negative repeatedly to keep myself safe.

However, my most significant failures never came from trying and missing the mark. The ones most difficult to accept were when I failed because I didn't try; when I did not put my hat in the ring, especially when I knew that it belonged there. That can be a hard pill to swallow. It is a betrayal of self, but on the bright side it is also an incredible lesson.

What will **not** trying do to you? Is that how regrets are born?

Reflection

The Wonderful Wizard of Oz is an American children's novel written by author L. Frank Baum. When I was young, I loved and feared the wicked witch of the west; she scared me silly.

I was certain that Dorothy and her little dog, Toto, were in danger the minute they left their home ("comfort zone"). Dorothy went to Oz and met the Scarecrow, Tin Man, and Lion on her journey along the Yellow Brick Road, for those that may not know the story. The Cowardly Lion searched for courage, the Tin Man desired a heart, and the Scarecrow wanted a brain.

Dorothy, meanwhile, was trying desperately to get back home. When the good witch tells Dorothy, "You've always had the power (to get home)," the Scarecrow asks, "Why didn't you tell her that before?" The witch gently responds, "Because she wouldn't have believed me; she had to learn it for herself!"

Isn't that everyone's story to some extent? Aren't we all on a similar yellow brick road, wanting to get home (or belong), afraid to leave our comfort zone yet driven to find and then express our courage, heart, and knowledge?

Perhaps for some, the road has been made more difficult. For instance, Dorothy had to withstand a tornado and being ripped away from those she knew and loved to learn that she "always" had the power within.

What do you have to do to learn this for yourself?

It is sad to negate ourselves. When you examine what is calling you and find that it spikes your "must-do meter," it probably should not be denied. Perhaps the timing isn't right now, but that is what bucket lists and goal-setting strategies are for.

See failures for what they are. Lessons and practice steps, helping you to climb to where you want to go. With each mistake, you can tweak your map because now you know what not to do.

So, the moral of this is to allow yourself to make mistakes—lots of them. My favorite feeling about this is: "Nine out of ten businesses fail. Some people hear that and think, why bother? Others hear it and think, I better start TEN businesses."

How would a person with an entrepreneurial spirit feel if they didn't even try?

Going Deeper

When you feel a pull in a certain direction, you should pay close attention and examine it.

- What are you feeling?
- Why are you feeling it?
- What is the worst thing that can happen if you decide to pursue the pull?
- How much energy does it take to resist the urge?

- Can you feel energized and free if you get behind it?

Failure is a step towards growth. For growth to be possible, you must reframe your thoughts about failure. What definition can you give to failure that will support growth? Is failure bad? No. It's just a lack of success—so far.

You can take what you've learned and keep going; appreciate that you are growing and that you're not just another spectator in life; continue to move forward and to throw your hat in the ring. When it lands, and it most certainly will, it will be all the sweeter for the effort you gave.

Negativity default

Try this now:

- Take out a piece of plain, white paper.
- Draw a dot smack in the middle of the paper.
- Stand back and look at the paper.
- What do you see?
- Do you only see the dot?

Ninety-eight percent of us will say, "I see a dot." Try it with a friend. Ask them if they see anything else on the entire sheet of paper. The majority will say that they only see the dot.

A friend of mine shared this exercise with me. At the time, he was running a drop-in shelter for the homeless. He also happens to be one of the most positive people I know. We talked about the many ways he tries to uplift his clients and how they/we all focus on negative thoughts and failures to a ridiculous degree.

The point is that the white of the paper becomes invisible to us. Yet, the paper's white represents all our successes, accomplishments, kindnesses given, and the things in life that we should celebrate and be grateful for.

Still, most of us will only focus on the dot. If you continue to focus on the dot (negative thoughts and failures), that is where you will reside. Can you accept that—or is it time for a change?

> *The most confident and successful people among us know that they will make mistakes. Sure, it bothers them, too. However, they quickly and decisively make a mental turn-around that shows their strong emotional muscle. It doesn't worry them less; they just brush it off faster.*

Everyone should have the opportunity to be heard. If you know your purpose in life, it will help compel you to use your voice. When you know your purpose, it helps ground you and sets you on your path. You'll have many important things to express. Permit yourself to be bold and brave in life. It is the only way to keep regrets at bay.

Remember Elizabeth from Chapter 4? She started to find

her unique voice as she continued to adjust her story about herself. She took strategic action. She got clear about what she wanted and now feels stronger in her body, stands straighter, looks people in the eyes, smiles more, and knows that what she has within her to share is as important as the next person's gifts. She knows that she matters.

If you have been traumatized by life circumstances, there is the fear that the issue will return. It is not unreasonable to believe that, because it did happen once. It makes sense to want to protect yourself from experiencing pain. It is smart.

What you don't want to do is to bury yourself in a state of victimhood. It is sad and always heartbreaking when bad things happen to good people. When it does happen, it becomes your job to overcome your circumstances. This has become part of your journey. As unfair as it is, you must put your healing first and get clear and strong so that you can overcome it! Otherwise, you can create negative habits, both in thinking and action, that become more difficult to rise above.

People can spend a lifetime hitting the same wall repeatedly. The hardest part of victimhood is recognizing that you are in the role of the victim in the first place. Ask yourself if you take responsibility for where you are right now in your life. If your mind immediately goes to "but my parents, my spouse, my boss" and more, you may want to dig a bit deeper or perhaps talk with a professional. Not that you are wrong, mind you, but you may be stuck.

A professional therapist can help guide you back to being you. Being a victim is self-limiting, and we all deserve better. It is a strength to reach out for help and stay with it until healing comes. That is why there are experts in crisis management called into schools and workplaces and for our first responders after a tragedy to help sort out the seemingly un-sortable. With the freedom of healing, your self-expression will arise with life-affirming hopefulness!

Now is the time to take the walls down. We need to listen more, especially to ourselves. Life coaches are taught that our clients are not broken and do not need fixing but that they hold the answers. When I was a new coach, I somewhat believed that. Now, I unequivocally believe it.

> *No one is ever a lost cause. It doesn't matter how confused or wounded you are; you can uplift your life to undreamed-of levels.*

We all know of someone who is wildly successful, yet knowing their history, we don't know how that could be. They grew up in poverty, suffered abuse and neglect, and still found their calling. They went on to live lives that appear to be unscathed by their earlier circumstances. The list of remarkable people and their accomplishments is truly endless. Perhaps the strife they went through gave them a resilience that they then used strategically.

To rise to that level of personal and professional success, they had to listen to themselves at a core level. Eventually, they create a place where the universe meets them and all of who they are becomes aligned. A place where the teachers present themselves; the mentors arrive, they find role models at every turn. This can happen for all of us! At our core, we can enter a new, more aware dimension.

Many believe that we are here to learn a lesson, perhaps more than one lesson. They believe that if we do not learn these lessons in this lifetime, we are fated to continue making the same mistakes in other lifetimes. The only way to stop this cyclic pattern is if we learn the lessons.

I coached a lovely woman with multiple degrees who felt stuck and angry. She continued to live in her parents' shadow and under her boyfriend's control. The view from my perspective is that her allowing it to happen was due to old generational stories. She was still trying to be the good girl and to please others. But at what cost?

It paints a picture of self-sacrifice and self-diminishment. A place where pain and anger are the only predictable results. If we stay in that angry place for too long, something will bubble up, like steam in a kettle, and potentially boil over.

She was aching to be herself and not to care what others thought of her. She was pining to do what she wanted to do when she wanted to do it, without encountering any disapproval or judgments.

She wanted her voice to matter! Why wasn't she being listened to?

126

Asking "why" is pure gold. It is the first step to an awareness that something doesn't have to be. The mind is questioning and trying to make sense of an embedded view. I inquired if she was willing to change her routine. We talked about cause and effect, that what she says and does will influence those around her. We also discussed how what she *doesn't* say or do has an equally powerful effect.

People can get a payoff for not speaking up. For one, they don't have to take responsibility for their thoughts. They can follow the crowd and not rock the boat. This way, they don't have to stand alone and be responsible for outcomes.

Not speaking our minds gives others permission to speak and make decisions for us, which can cause underlying anger on both sides. If we don't take responsibility for ourselves, we can place a heavy and sometimes unfair burden on others.

Remember the stone being tossed into the pond and the ripple effect? Your actions and lack of actions influence others. What's more, the stone makes room for YOU to take your rightful place!

Taking responsibility is the only mature choice.

Finding your voice takes maturity, and it is a choice you must consciously make. Perhaps the most important stand to make in life is to love and accept yourself, flaws and all. In today's vernacular, it's adulting!

Exercise

Learning to express ourselves is an ongoing process, and it's easier to start the process with what we already know. Try answering the questions below in your head, out loud or on paper, and feel good about voicing who you are.

- What excites you?
- What angers you?
- What do you feel compelled to talk about, see, and do?
- Who do you respect and why?
- Who, dead or alive, do you want to sit and chat with? (Think of your ultimate mentor.)
- Can you make some strategic changes and stretch yourself for more?
- How can you contribute?

Can you imagine living your life without expressing yourself? Oh, the regrets. It doesn't matter the genre you choose to express yourself. It just matters that you DO. Leave no stone untossed, because life happens from and in those ripples.

Summary

Learning to listen to ourselves will help us identify what we really want out of life, and then we must learn how to express our desires and achieve those needs and wants.

Chapter 8

FORGIVENESS

Introduction

Forgiveness could very well be the key to freedom. Once you understand just how beneficial forgiveness is for your happiness and success, you'll be jumping through hoops to let your grievances go.

The alternative to not forgiving yourself can be a lifetime of guilt and despair. None of us deserve to be living from guilt, fear, and self-inflicted oppression. That is an unhealthy and lost place to be. Truly, once you get clear about your intentions (what you want) in life, it can become a more-straightforward-than-expected thing to do.

Forgiving ourselves can sometimes be more difficult than forgiving others. Some of the most paralyzing words you can say are, "I will never forgive myself for when I did this or that." You may truly believe that you can never forgive yourself. However, this belief is no more than a thought, and we know you can change your thoughts. Let's try to figure out how to change this one.

Perhaps you did some stupid, embarrassing stuff or even a terrible thing or two. What you need to understand is that at any given time, you can only do *What. You. Know. How. To. Do.* That *then* was a completely different time and place in your life, not the time and place you live in today! *Then* you were reacting unconsciously to the feelings, values, and circumstances that were in your environment.

You are human. We all make mistakes at the level of our awareness.

You were surrounded by different situations, some of which may have been created by you, or they may have been completely beyond your control. You were an unaware and even an imperfect human being reacting to your circumstances in the only way you knew how! If you were responding with fear, you were in lower-level feelings, and regrets can often follow.

When responding with love, we are in our higher-level feelings. This is our destination, where good things happen. Sometimes the simplest explanation and view really resonates because it makes the most sense.

Offering and receiving forgiveness is complicated because of the layers of pain, betrayal, humiliation, and anger that can be associated with what occurred. Whether you are the one to forgive or be forgiven, you will have your inner work to do. There will be a release of some kind that will need to be sorted through. To forgive or be forgiven by others will help you to unpack your pain.

In most cases, the person that hurt you couldn't show up in the way you needed them to. They were not able to be the parent, sibling, partner, co-worker, friend you needed, just as you were sometimes not able to be there for others—or even for yourself.

This can lead to unprocessed pain being locked inside somewhere. Perhaps you feel it in your shoulders, neck, back, belly? Some studies have raised the possibility that stress may cause autoimmune diseases, such as lupus or rheumatoid arthritis (to name a few) because they found a higher incidence of autoimmune diseases among people who were previously diagnosed with stress-related disorders.

Picture a balloon over-extended or steam escaping a kettle—something's got to give!

In my lifetime, I've known a handful of people that are quick to anger. They are ultra-sensitive. A look, a word or even a sigh can set them off. It is almost as though they have exposed nerve endings. Their feelings are raw, exposed and always primed to respond. They make an impression, get people to take notice and to walk on eggshells. Their anger serves them—although it doesn't feel good, and it alienates them from others.

It is sad that hurt people often hurt other people. It explains so well generational pain.

If this resonates with you and unhealed pain still haunts you, even after many years, isn't it best to move mountains to heal it?

To move on in life, pain must be released. It takes not only awareness but also an inner strength to be able to process an acute feeling. It is important to allow yourself the time and space needed to sort through any trauma. If it remains ruminating inside, you can keep being triggered by this feeling repeatedly.

There are abhorrent offenses that will never be okay with you/us and society. Deviant people and actions could have affected you, your loved ones, or the world at large. I believe that hurtful, horrible situations and the people that create those situations need to be stopped, even sometimes removed from society for the safety of others.

However, regardless of whether they are dealt with by the law or not, we can continue to be victimized by events, not of our making. Yes, it is damn unfair that something was a significant event in your life, and now you are *forced* to deal with it. I'm an empath, and I understand that the more sensitive you are, the harder it can be to heal. The question arises: "Why me?"

> *Eventually, with wisdom and age, the question is more about how can you move on and rise above to become whole and happy.*

Forgiving someone who has hurt you takes courage, and sometimes being at the end of your rope! You may fear that you will feel the abuse all over again. You can think that they will get away scot-free. But they have their side of things to deal with, and that is not your problem.

What can we do with the kind of nearly impossible situations to forgive because They...Are...So...Wrong? Perhaps you can say:

Here God, universe, source—I cannot carry this any longer. I now release it to you. I don't want to keep revisiting it. I accept that these people, circumstances, ideologies were built on an unhealthy and, in some cases, abusive foundation. But, hey, it and they are above my ability to cope with, so here...

If I do revisit, I will continue to release it to you and let it go (quickly) until I feel free from it—which is what I want. Thank you.

You can create your version of the above words, write them (or other feelings), and burn the paper. You should then celebrate taking your power back.

Sarah's Story

Alcoholics Anonymous (AA) was founded in 1935 by Bill Wilson and Dr. Robert Smith. Their successful twelve-step program is used to help alcoholics and addicts overcome shame and guilt as they work to beat their addictions. Each step lists something they've achieved and maintained for sobriety.

Steps eight and nine are focused on forgiveness:

- Made a list of persons we had harmed and

became willing to make amends to them all.

- Made direct amends to such people wherever possible, except when to do so would injure them or others.

I received a heartfelt apology from my friend, Sarah, who made amends while following these steps. I must say, I have never received nor felt such an honest and deep apology. Had it been superficial, I would have felt that energy as well.

Her offering the apology and its heartfelt truth should have set her—or anyone else that does the same work—free. It was such an impactful and sincere way to ask for forgiveness. You can "feel" the truth of sincerity. What more can a person do than to offer their truth?

Once she gave her apology, it became my prerogative whether to accept it. I can tell you that it felt wonderful to receive it. I didn't clap back at her and tell her how many ways she had hurt me, although giving an apology leaves people vulnerable to that possibility.

Thankfully, I didn't need to take that tack; however, be aware that the person you hurt may indeed need the space to have their say!

It takes growth, maturity and bravery to give and accept a heartfelt apology, which is exactly why it can be life changing.

Reflection

Although I am not an expert in the twelve steps, the fact that the steps are still impactful is evidence of their effectiveness. I have been an admirer of this program and those who continue to live a sober life.

Forgiving yourself is a gift to *you*. By apologizing to me, Sarah also sought self-forgiveness. She wanted to set herself free from the guilt and shame she carried by past words and deeds. Had I not forgiven her—well, then, that would be about me, not her. She was doing her work! She offered me the gift of understanding why she did what she did, etc., and how her actions, hurtful at the time, were not about me; they were about her. Her explicit apology gave me insight into myself as well as her and helped set me free.

As Sarah released her guilt and shame, she created an opportunity for a brighter future. She built a healthy foundation for herself that could maintain a lasting change. She was hindered but found a path forward to health, growth, and the pursuit of happiness. What a gift!

I believe that you deserve the peace that letting go of guilt and shame can bring to you.

What if I'm the one who needs forgiveness?

Sarah had to acknowledge that her actions and words had hurt people. Her understanding of that truth was the first step for her. Truth is hard to acknowledge, especially when one usually hides behind their pain. Again, we know that hurt people hurt people. It is unfortunate but also very true. We also know that some people that have been hurt can become the kindest people on the planet—because they know what it feels like to be hurt.

Hurt people have been victims. As a result, they can stay stuck in a victim mentality far beyond the time that they are being hurt.

Victimhood permits people a kind of entitlement—a permission to transfer all kinds of dysfunction to others. There are so many layers to victimhood. A victim receives sympathy from others, deservedly so at one time, but, of course, the need for sympathy should end as one grows and matures. However, if one doesn't grow and mature, they can keep looking for sympathy and ways to use their victimhood to get what they need and want.

I believe that this concept is a significant one for people to understand. This is a form of transference. Therefore, it behooves all of us to understand that quality of life for all of us matters. Each person, group, town, city, country deserves to have their needs met in healthy ways.

We will all grow and benefit by lifting each other. We are all connected, we all transfer, and the results are felt at every level of our lives.

Going Deeper

So, what can we do to help forgive ourselves or others?

Acknowledge your actions

Sarah didn't make excuses or sugarcoat her actions in any way. She accepted complete responsibility. She asked for forgiveness and felt sincere regret for her actions.

Accepting what you've done, understanding why you did it, and committing to changing your ways is essential. However, it's also important to move on and stop continually beating yourself up over things you can't change.

In the same way, you need to separate the harm done to you from the harm you're perpetuating by holding onto the hurt, instead of forgiving.

Take responsibility

Remember that you can't force someone to forgive you. Others need to move to forgiveness at their own pace. In this life step, you need to allow them space. Whatever happens, just do you and commit to living a life of compassion, empathy, and respect for others.

However, you can forgive yourself, and if that's what's needed, take a deep breath and allow yourself to accept the past and move on to a better future.

Commit to respect

What if the person I'm forgiving doesn't change?

If a person doesn't change, remember that it has nothing to do with you. We are all in different places. If they are part of your everyday life and are a source of continued pain, you will have to decide. You don't need another's permission or agreement to feel the benefits of forgiveness.

Plus, that is not the point of forgiveness. The point is to release you from being pulled back into negative feelings and open a space to receive more joy, peace, and freedom to be the person you want to be.

Some believe we live many lives and that we are supposed to learn an important lesson during each lifetime. Others say, "You only have one life."

Well, whichever way we believe, we know for sure that we will only live this *life once*. Ask yourself what you may need to learn in this lifetime. Ponder this for a spell.

Forgiveness can help us live an extraordinary life while we are here. It breaks down walls that hinder progress. It creates an opening for more positivity, fosters wellness, and builds unshakable confidence.

Let's be fanciful and imagine how a person looks while wearing forgiveness. Would you expect an easy smile and clear eyes (clarity), great posture (grounded-ness), a happy lightness, and unrestrained forward motion (Gremlins under control)?

Or how about we create an even more fanciful visual? The calm after the storm; the beauty of springtime around the world when plants bloom, allowing for their glorious colors to burst forth unhindered; the grass is green and lush; the sky is blue; the birds are freely soaring.

Wouldn't you rather nurture your power and energy for your conscious use? Where will more power and energy take you? Letting go of the past through forgiveness and moving forward is the only way to achieve this freedom.

If this chapter is resonating with you, there is a reason. This is your time. You may want to think seriously about taking steps to forgive yourself and others.

Exercise

What have you done in your life that you feel you need forgiveness for? Who do you need to talk to? Write to? How can you accept what you've done and forgive yourself? Is there anything you feel you need to do to make amends?

Who in your life do you need to forgive? What is holding you back? Are you giving your power and energy to those that do not deserve it? Consider that negative feeling as a wall keeping you confined. Making a conscious decision to forgive someone who hurt you and no longer allowing them to affect you can be incredibly freeing.

Summary

Forgiveness is done for our own sake, not for the sake of the person being forgiven.

Forgiving ourselves is just as important as forgiving others. It has been shown to decrease depression, anxiety, unhealthy anger, and the symptoms of PTSD. A decrease in emotional stress and pain can lead to a physically healthier life as well.

Forgiveness allows us to move on in the most empowered of ways. It is the key to freedom because we consciously let go of limiting beliefs (thoughts) and feelings.

Chapter 9

GRATITUDE

Introduction

The practice of gratitude opens our eyes to the magic that makes up our world. It unlocks stuck minds and brings a rush of positive thoughts that can bring us love and connection. It can turn doubts into possibilities, which can turn into goals. They can then turn into accomplishments, which can turn into success. Having success can turn into prosperity, therefore, giving people an option of giving back, which can help make the world a kinder place, which can bring everyone happiness.

And all this massive energy is because of appreciation!

> *Practicing gratitude is a wake-up call and an excellent truth serum, especially for those that tend to wallow in yesterday and fixate on the negative.*

Practicing gratitude is a form of mindfulness that promotes all areas of health: mind, body, and spirit. It is a proven modality that stimulates positivity, and positivity brings us to our higher-level emotions.

When you are grateful, you cannot hold onto negative feelings. You can't be sad or angry and thankful at the same time. It just doesn't work that way.

Many in the mindfulness community, authors, and life coaches have described gratitude as a natural feeling that comes from within. Others describe being grateful or ungrateful as a choice. I fall right smack between both definitions.

I realized that if I wasn't practicing gratitude, it was because I was fixating on the past. What I now understand is that appreciation naturally surfaces for emotionally healthy people. If there is a lot of chaos and noise, it is simply harder for a person to feel grateful.

Whether being grateful surfaces organically for you or you need to make a concerted effort to find it, the payoff is worth the effort! You can look carefully at all that was, and is, terrific in your life. Just pivoting your thoughts slightly from what you don't have to all that you do have will help you. You may realize that you have much to be grateful for.

I was tempted to skip this chapter because this practice is as unique as the people reading this page, but I want to bring a universal feel to the subject. To grasp the benefits of gratitude, we must take age, gender, culture, and experiences into account.

With science now vouching about the advantages of practicing gratitude, there are more suggestions than ever about how to express and feel it.

In my experience, gratitude is the great equalizer of our troubles. No matter the hurt, pain, or fear you experience in your life, there is always something for which to be grateful.

The intangibles make life worth living and the many pressing and sometimes scary issues worth solving.

Gratitude supports:

- Happiness
- Self-love
- Love of others
- Creativity
- Productivity
- Reflection
- Better sleep
- Healthier immune system
- Compassion
- Goal setting and achieving
- Better friendships
- Happier children
- Happier parents

- Stronger family units
- And so much more!

Going Deeper

Try telling yourself the statements below at least once a day. If you are stuck, and this practice is difficult for you, then start wherever you can.

I am grateful that I can:

- Walk
- Talk
- Buy food
- Have loved ones
- Have a roof over my head

Go back to basics. Keep adding more and more to this list because consciously focusing on what you have to be grateful for will bring you closer to the higher-level feelings you are aiming for. As a reminder, higher-level feelings lead to better outcomes in all aspects of life!

Children can take things for granted unless appreciation is modeled or taught. If their days and life are going well, i.e., they have a safe place to land, food, respect, love, and connection, all will go a long way to setting the stage for being grateful. Happiness and higher levels of emotion tend to bubble up naturally for children. *This is the energy field where children are most apt to develop their self-confidence and belief in themselves.*

Most children have not yet built the walls and blocks that can limit their beliefs and lives, and we do not want these limitations for them!

As an aside, children surrounded by dysfunction absorb that energy and can take on the blame for what is happening. Living in those circumstances will block true gratitude from organically emerging. The noise that the dysfunction creates for them will always take center stage, and all this may make healthy choices unimaginable for them.

The way to avoid this is to model a gratitude lifestyle and be conscious of what you are presenting to your children.

Anger begets anger and anxiety, etc.

Joy begets joy and promotes wellbeing, etc.

If you have modeled negative emotions and traits, regardless of the reasons, then begin creating positive change. It is never too late to start now, but you must stay steadfast in these efforts. *If the predictor of past behavior is the predictor of future behavior, it is reasonable to understand that others will need time to trust in it even though you feel the change inside.*

Healthy rituals promote a stronger body and mind. Imagine you can magnify your strengths by *practicing* gratitude—isn't that what confidence looks and feels like?

What other small rituals besides practicing gratitude can you put in place to impact your life for the better?

What we appreciate will change as we grow and evolve.

What are you grateful for?

Exercise

Below are several different ways to help us express gratitude. Start with one and see where it takes you.

- Journal
- Meditate
- Pray
- Enjoy nature
- Thank everyone
- Pay it forward
- Apologize
- Do favors
- Compliment
- Listen
- Give meaningful gifts (they can be small)
- Show respect
- Be charitable

What would you add to the list?

There is so much more than you can do to show appreciation for your life. Any means of gratitude can change your life exponentially. If you make this a ritual, you will likely improve an untold number of lives (including yours) without even realizing it.

Summary

You can see a beautiful flower, sunset, ocean, meadow, etc., with your eyes. There is much to be grateful for when you are looking at and experiencing the beauty of nature.

To practice gratitude, you can uplift your spirit and put yourself in a positive feeling space.

Seeing is believing...feeling can be life changing. Remember that you cannot see love or energy, but you can feel them! Gratitude helps you reach that positive place and stay there.

Chapter 10

MEETING SIX HUMAN NEEDS

Introduction

Would you like to know why you do what you do? Why others do what they do? How can you strategically make positive, lasting change?

Understanding the Six Human Needs will intensify mindfulness for yet another layer of clarity that can speed the course of empowerment and change.

The Six Human Needs

Needs of the personality:

- Certainty
- Uncertainty
- Significance
- Love and Connection

Needs of the spirit:

- Growth
- Contribution

When I first learned about our Six Human Needs, my mind became open to a deeper understanding of all human nature. It was an aha moment for me. I got it! Of course, we have human needs, and then, of course, they are universal. This awareness brings a powerful understanding of ourselves and others. I became fascinated by how this knowledge can help us heal and create a path to what we truly desire.

Especially important is how we feed our lower-and higher-level emotions with these needs because that helps us better understand why we continue to do things that are both beneficial and not beneficial for us.

This is powerful.

The Six Human Needs are universal! These needs drive your feelings and actions and those of your partners, children, friends, teachers, employers, politicians, community leaders—everyone.

Knowing which needs are the most important to you will tell you a lot about yourself. How you meet them is what creates your outcome. Understanding your needs tell you why you are compelled to do certain things in a certain way. How you choose to meet your needs can simply be life changing.

Whether we meet them in good/healthy ways or not-so-good ways, meet them we will! One thing's certain: we Will. Meet. Our. Needs.

It has been a lifelong quest of mine to understand human nature. My Strategic Intervention (SI) life coach training is through Robbins-Madanes Coach Training™. My teachers were Mark and Magali Peysha, and I am grateful to have had the opportunity to learn from them. I am equally grateful to my other coaching programs, teachers and mentors, whose lessons and influence are within the pages of this book as well.

What distinguishes SI from other strategic studies is the belief that certain holistic solutions "snap into place" when more of a person's needs are met, expressed, and elevated. These solutions deliver more benefits for less effort.

The Six Human Needs theory is modeled on the work of Anthony Robbins, in collaboration with Cloe Madanes, (SI) founders Mark and Magali Peysha. Their work has been influenced by the great insights and works of Victor Frankl and Milton Erickson's creative breakthroughs in human intervention.

Tony Robbins discusses the invisible forces that motivate everyone's action in his Ted Talk "Why we do what we do", which is well worth our time!

What can make us different: age, culture, gender, environment, education, foods, appearance, religion, etc.

What makes us alike: our human needs, emotions, physicality, etc.

We have Six Human Needs that influence our deepest motivations and determine how we prioritize our decisions and actions.

Let's look closer at the Six Human Needs.

The first four are referred to as the needs of the personality, as they are centered around our pursuit of *self-fulfillment and achievement.*

Needs of the personality

Certainty

- The need for safety, security, comfort, order, consistency, and control. At a basic level, each of us must satisfy a core sense of stability in our world.

Variety

- The need for uncertainty, diversity, challenge, change, surprise, and adventure.

These first two human needs work as polarities with each other—seemingly opposing forces that together make a whole. When we are out of balance with one (e.g., so certain that we are bored), it is often the other (e.g., a dose of something new) that brings us back into balance.

Significance

- The need for meaning, validation, feeling needed, honored, wanted, and special. When we find significance within (purpose), we don't require approval from others.

Love & Connection

- The need for connection, communication, intimacy, and shared love with others.

There are extremes in life. Just as with mindfulness, we have love and fear as opposites; with the Six Human Needs, it becomes how extreme or balanced your needs are.

For instance, if you have a strong need for significance/feeling important/unique, that's quite fine because we all have that need. These are all needs that you will meet one way or another. Someone else might find their need for certainty is stronger, while another might find the need for variety outweighs others.

Once you understand your needs, you may question how well you are meeting them. Are you extreme, balanced, enthusiastic? Are you meeting your needs in ways that open doors to progress, or are you shutting down because your energy is evaporating as you meet your needs in unhealthy ways?

How can you feel significant, for example? Perhaps it's by the degrees you've received, the job title you hold, the nonprofits you volunteer for, the amount of money you make, how you look, the car you drive, the lives you save as a nurse/doctor, the church you pastor—significance can come to us in many ways.

Robbins has asked: If a gang member puts a gun to a person's head, who becomes the most significant person in the room? Powerful, right?

How would holding someone's life in his hands fulfill some of that gang member's human needs?

- He meets his need for *significance* by becoming the most important person in the room.

- He experiences *variety*, a rush, and a thrill from controlling someone's life.

- He experiences *certainty* as well because he knows for certain the gun would get results.

We can be certain that we will meet our needs one way or another, and it's best if we meet them in positive and healthy ways!

Understanding the needs of the personality offer valuable information about the causes of addiction. This knowledge can support preventive measures by offering a clear understanding why a person may choose a substance and why a sober person may be triggered back to self-medicate. This understanding can help them to remain substance-free by knowing how to meet/soothe their needs differently.

153

Why does someone become addicted? How can we create lasting change away from an addiction?

My story

There have been times in my life when I've had a clear-cut awareness. Learning about the Six Human Needs is one of those times!

I was once highly addicted to smoking cigarettes. I "emotionally and physically" felt and lived the power of that addiction daily. It engulfed me. I scheduled smoking into my day. Quitting for good, well, it seemed like an impossible feat.

After years of trying, I finally quit. I did not know that I was self-medicating and filling my needs by smoking. This wasn't a conscious choice for me. I'd like to see these human needs taught in ever expanding circles. I think that learning them could benefit young families, and recovery specialists alike, by identifying an instrumental cause/trap of addition. The needs can be an effective resource for preventing unhealthy ways to soothe lower-level feelings.

We are human, we have voids to fill, why not learn to fill them in healthy ways?

> *If you're focused on at least three out of the four personality needs to get through the day, you will become addicted to whatever specific thing or action you are using to meet your needs.*

Thoughts on addiction

Addiction is caused by how we meet our human needs. How so?

I can predict with confidence that each former or current smoker will agree with at least three of the following:

- As a smoker, I felt *certainty* that my cigarettes would always be there for me. They would not yell at me, frown at me, or offer me any attitude. I would get what I needed from the nicotine, self-medicate, and feel a certain way.

- I also got *variety* from how slow or quickly I inhaled. If I wanted to feel energized, I would smoke quickly. If I needed to relax, I inhaled slowly.

- I may have started smoking to be cool/ *significant* and hang with my smoking friends. Most of us that smoke start at a young age.

- I can't tell you how often I have heard that a smoker *loves* their cigarettes, and they are their best friend (*love and connection*). I also loved and felt connected to smoking— until I didn't any longer!

As I understand the Six Human Needs, smoking fulfilled all four needs of the personality for me. Again, per the teachings, had I met three of these needs by smoking, I would be addicted. Well, I met all four personality

155

needs, and quitting smoking was brutal! Until it wasn't!

Perhaps had I been raised to understand these needs, I may have been able to avoid smoking. In addition, had I known about them during my smoking years, it may have helped speed up the quitting process. I could have worked to consciously meet my needs in healthier ways.

As I mentioned, I found quitting difficult. I tried and failed many times until finally, it did happen. Breaking patterns linked to self-medication and addiction are hard, sometimes too hard. The layers of help/healing and awareness must first be set in place.

We know that lower-level feelings and wounds can lead to self-medicating. Being able to pinpoint which needs are the most important for a person to meet can be enlightening. It answers questions that can support the avoidance of addictions and then strongly support those in recovery to live a life free from addictions.

You can replace my addiction to cigarettes with almost anything—drugs, alcohol, food, tattoos, piercings, exercise, nail-biting, work, gambling, technology, exercise, phones, video games—virtually anything that is a distraction from not feeling terrific and gives a "human-need fix."

When we do the work and free ourselves from an addiction, we must replace all of those needs that it was meeting with something else.

Consider if one takes opioids and has become addicted.

- The medication could meet a need for certainty as the drug of choice helps one feel calm, safe, and pain-free.

- It can meet a need for variety as the feelings they feel change, giving them a rush/high, a low, and many feelings in between.

- Perhaps they can even feel a sense of significance because their friends are in this unique/different way of life with them. They feel accepted within this community.

- And lastly, they can feel love and connection, as the drug is their connection to a community and an intended feeling/fix. Their emotions and body feel much better—and for a time, all is right with the world.

Until it all goes very wrong!

When I finally quit smoking, it was unquestionably one of the best decisions for the health of my mind, body, and spirit. I had felt trapped, embarrassed, and out of control by smoking. I finally pulled free and quickly gained fifteen pounds! I didn't know that I had to relearn how to meet my needs in healthier ways. Because remember, meet them we will! Perhaps this knowledge may have helped me to replace unhealthy eating choices with better choices!

With awareness, you can ask yourself questions about how well you are meeting your needs. Which needs resonate most for you? For those raising children, teaching, or in the world of service to humankind, we instinctively know the importance of meeting human needs healthily.

Needs of the spirit

In human needs psychology, the final two needs are defined as "needs of the spirit."

Growth

- The need for physical, emotional, intellectual, and spiritual development. People are most happy when they are evolving.

Contribution

- The need to give, care, protect beyond ourselves, serve others for the good of all—using our purpose, happily being in our zone, fulfilling our own needs by contributing to others.

Satisfying the needs of the spirit is where we will find fulfillment.

Growth and Contribution are where our purpose and cumulative wisdom are activated—almost seamlessly! It's where we meet and meld all our human needs simultaneously. It is the space where we are growing and sharing and being at one with our gifts.

Reflection

If we meet our need for certainty at a comfortable level, we are feeling safe. This safety can allow for peace of mind and physical comfort.

It can also make it hard for some of us to step outside of this comfort zone and continue to grow. Being stuck, procrastinating, and holding yourself back can all be very boring and make for a very dull life.

> *Growth should be the aim! If we are not growing, we are dying.*

Is it time for you to make a life transition, to grow and transform? The truth is you can remain too long in a comfort zone. If you do, you may miss the very best experiences that life can offer. Stepping out of your comfort zone means engaging in things that you don't naturally feel comfortable doing. I encourage you to push yourself to meet your needs in more healthy and challenging ways. Do things that you wouldn't normally do. Be bold with your gifts!

When we attempt to step out of our comfort zone, we can think of all the things that can go wrong. Alarm bells ring, and then our old stories resurface. These stories can end all that remarkable creativity and passion that was about to burst forth.

Another reason it is hard to move out of our comfort zone is because we have already used so much grit and energy to get to where we are. In many cases, it was quite hard to get to this place of certainty. But you must remember that you've built *resilience* during the climb.

> *It is important to understand that each stage of growth eventually gets easier. Each time you move forward, you will have all the experience and wisdom you have acquired at previous stages to assist you.*

Moving outside your comfort zone will help you to be more focused and creative. It creates energy and encourages productivity. Your skills and innate strengths come alive and are honed for success. Hey, it's also where the fun is!

We want to up-level our lives, but we can feel less certainty when we move out of our comfort zone. We are taking a risk, and this can be an invitation to our Gremlins! When triggered we can even feel physical changes come over us. Are these feelings we feel that of anxiety or excitement? Which one is the greatest thought/feeling to feed?

Imagine you can feed the excitement (rather than the anxiety) and consciously enjoy this feeling of growth.

Just remind yourself that you don't need to start from scratch. You have learned quite a bit about what works and what doesn't work. Take the leap—just take it!

You can now bring what you know to your next set of goals. You will acquire even more skills and wisdom as you achieve these new objectives and create a pattern for growth and success. There will always be a next time, another goal to chase. That's life; that is what we are meant to do. Grow, have fun, transform, be. Just keep upping the ante.

> *Learning new things throughout your life contributes to confidence, happiness, and excitement. Breakthroughs and transformation are found by being and doing more than you ever thought possible; so are happiness and success!*

Going Deeper

Entertainer Beyoncé Knowles has an alter ego named Sasha Fierce, who Beyoncé becomes when she goes on stage. She doesn't just "think" of herself as Sasha Fierce and perform. Beyoncé has done her work, honed her craft, and when she steps out, she calls on a very real part of herself to push through her fears and discomfort to reach a goal.

Like the rest of us, Beyoncé has her talents and gifts honed and ready to go. I assume that your talents are different, and you may or may not be a global superstar. However, don't doubt that you do have superpowers as well. Beyoncé found a way to face her fear and do what she is meant to do. It cannot be a coincidence that Sasha's last name is Fierce. There is power in that word. She uses it well and has shared/contributed her technique with us. How generous and inspiring!

It can be helpful to know that you, too, have many parts of yourself that you can call upon when needed. (e.g., the parent, child, leader, warrior, teacher, lover, light-hearted one, executive, admin, and more.)

Sometimes, parts of our personalities can be all-encompassing, and some other parts need a little strengthening. An example of too honed could be someone that brings their warrior, executive, or leader into their home 24/7 when perhaps it would be much more fun if they brought their warm and fuzzy side home instead. Awareness, again, being conscious of how we show up!

The most successful people use each set point they reach as a launching pad to their next set of goals. Think of a set point as a stair. Each time they have arrived and land on one stair, they celebrate their newest accomplishment. They take stock, look around and map out where they want to go or what they want to do next. Then they take action!

You can do this too. It is a great model to follow. Each of your accomplishments is real and has provided you with new skills, experience, and wisdom to make your next move forward so much easier. When you are consciously making decisions, you can be strategic about your choices. You have more innate talents fortifying you and compelling you forward than you may know.

When you create your next goal (hopefully, it's a big one), you will create action steps to follow. You will consciously manage your next steps. This big goal will up-level your life somehow, potentially bringing you and yours to a new standard of living.

One final caveat: Get grounded! Deciding to act means you just invited your Gremlins to pay you a visit.

Exercise

Here are two ways to set aside fear and begin stretching your "growth muscles" to reach for more in your life.

Step 1: What Are Your Needs?

The questions below will help you start thinking about and prioritizing your needs so it's easier to begin meeting them.

- What two needs are the most important to you?
- How do you meet them?
- Which needs do you want to focus on more?
- How can you bring more balance into your life?

Step 2: Steps for Meeting Those Needs

- Think about everything that can go right. Close your eyes and visualize yourself living your dreams. What are you doing? Sit with that image until you believe in it.

- Create a vision board and infuse it with everything you want your life to be, have, and hold. Journal your dreams until you believe every word is possible. (Because it is!)

- Put together a group of proactive and like-minded people who want to stretch and grow too. Hold each other accountable for taking those critical next steps. Have each member strategically create their visual to depict each opportunity and dream right outside their comfort zone.

- Listen for the whispers and calls inside of you to do more. If specific thoughts keep resurfacing, there is a reason.

Make a pact with yourself to strive for more. Resist the easiest path. What if your biggest challenge results in you reaching your goals and your dreams coming true? You have this one life, that much you know for sure. Don't wait for life to come to you. Meet your life head-on and with purpose. Move each day in the direction of your goals and dreams. Remember as well that if you have young eyes watching you, double your efforts to claim your success.

Summary

The four needs of the personality—*Certainty, Variety, Significance,* and *Love and Connection*—can be the keys to unlocking addictions and replacing them with healthier solutions. They are also the keys to understanding why we do what we do and how we can strategically strive for more in our lives.

The two needs of the spirit—*Growth and Contribution*—are the keys to unlocking spiritual peace and fulfillment.

Consider how helpful it is to have this knowledge not only of your human needs but those of others as well. Always remember that your children have these ever-changing needs too!

Chapter 11

ARCHETYPES

Introduction

There is a lot written about the patterns, wisdom (positive and negative), strengths, and weaknesses found within our archetypes. Also, much is written about the power that comes from integrating them consciously.

There are archetypes like CEO, Warrior, Leader, Goofball, Lover, Teacher, Helper, Magician, and so many more. It is normal to have these varying parts of ourselves—and more powerful than we know.

> *The key is to use our strengths with an awareness and consciousness that lets the very best of them/us show up. These ever-evolving parts of ourselves make us more complex, complete, and powerful.*

Instinctively we have always known of them, though we used them unconsciously. The real power comes when we become conscious of how to integrate all our parts.

Bob's Journey: Warrior Archetype

Bob came to coaching because of a personal and professional crisis. His world, as he knew it, was on the verge of collapsing. His marriage seemed to be doomed. His wife was a successful woman he loved dearly, but he found that may not be enough. They had been striving for financial security, and in unequal measures, family happiness. They have two small children.

He met most of his needs for security, variety, significance, and connection at work, until, due to a dispute with his business partners, he decided to sell his share of the business and start over again. Suddenly he felt lost. These challenges are where we started to unravel what had happened and find out where the blinders were for this perfect storm to occur in the first place.

We started with some strength work and revisited his talents, work history, and gifts. First things first: we needed to build a foundation with an authentic sense of stability for him before we could move forward. He came alive when we talked about his gifts and accomplishments. His posture became straighter, more robust. His face relaxed as he remembered his true self.

The recent breakdown of his work life allowed him to focus on his home life and marriage. Since his needs weren't being met at work, all the attention he had focused on work moved to the next best thing. In this case, his marriage.

Is this what I want in a relationship?

Is this what she wants?

Of course, his wife wasn't ready for this level of attention to their marriage and family life! She was also unconsciously filling her needs in the best way she knew how. His wife kept her focus on work and their children.

Bob being at loose ends, unexpectedly opened both of their eyes. The only direction for both was forward, improving their life balance and quality of life.

We discussed how we have these different "parts" of ourselves. Some parts may lie dormant, some can be front and center, and other parts of ourselves we may flow in and out of smoothly, or not so smoothly, throughout our lives.

I asked Bob if he would be willing to do some archetype work with me. I explained that it could be incredibly powerful.

Bob's an intense guy, but he didn't appear to be at the first meeting. He is fit and appears hard-wired for success. He had some quick insights, which can happen in coaching as we transfer and broaden our focus. Each process and conversation gave him a new insight into why he and others do what they do—and did what they did. He's a proactive person and wanted to take these lessons forward.

Bob continues to process what he learns while simultaneously taking action. He is the type of person who, when he makes a decision, acts swiftly. I asked him what part of himself he would like to converse with and get to know better. The goal was to gain insights and a new source of strength. He chose well. He wanted to work with his Warrior and Magician parts.

My clients determine if the archetypes we are working with are masculine or feminine. We all have both traits. One of my clients recently shared that their Warrior is androgynous. The gender question can create further awareness of the energy and patterns within our archetypes.

When I first do this work with a client, we create a sacred place for the client's comfort, make a pact for discovery, and become a reliable team. Together we get centered, and then off we go.

At this point, I spoke to his Warrior only. I asked his Warrior how he has shown up for Bob. It turns out that his Warrior had been dormant lately. Bob started to remember vividly that his Warrior had been front and center when he began his business, when he turned his talents and gifts into a financial success, when he asked his wife to marry him, when he built a home, when he overcame a speech impediment, when he survived bullying, and throughout his formal education.

Archetype work is powerful. The strength work we did previously became a strong foundation for this work to excel. Talking to one's Warrior can magnify the impact because both are important. The strength work reminded Bob of his accomplishments. It put him into a neutral space. The goal with the strength work is to soothe and empower the vulnerable parts. In Bob's case, it put him in a more vital, receptive state of mind. He was no longer feeling lost. He was neutral, open and ready to expand his footing.

The archetype work reminded him that he has parts of himself (states of being) that he had called on to achieve many accomplishments. This understanding of self then brought him swiftly to a new level of strength and confidence. We can identify and call upon parts of ourselves when we need or want to. We can integrate them and flow between them just by knowing they are within us.

By the time we integrated his Warrior, we had an impressive list of the ways his Warrior had shown up for him.

After the work, Bob thanked his Warrior for how he had shown up for him when he had needed an extra oomph throughout his life. This was powerful and enlightening for him. He felt happy and hopeful. The archetype process uncovered a personal development tool that he can consciously use moving forward—along with some well-deserved pride. He purposely asked his Warrior to be more present and available to him.

Archetypes and Energy

Typically, when our Warrior comes out, we are digging deep into our being. Our motivation and focus are at an all-time high. Knowing for sure that our Warrior has our back can help us to:

- Stop procrastinating
- Build motivation
- Move mountains
- Lift cars!

Now, the Warrior can be intense, right? We've heard about people lifting cars off others or catching a child falling out of a building, not to mention the Warriors that show up daily by way of our first responders! I'm sure adrenaline plays a role as well. This energy provides us with a power source of fuel that can help us to fulfill our purpose, achieve excellence, and leave a legacy.

The unconscious use of this energy can have a polarizing effect. A consciously kind and compassionate Warrior's energy can power change that transcends all harm. In contrast, an unconscious Warrior's energy can sometimes create harm, even if it's unintentional. The Warrior wears the same cloth as both sinners and saints.

How do we transition our Warrior for calmer situations? Perhaps we create an intimate awareness and friendship with ourselves and all the parts of us?

We can have dominant archetypes. We all know caregivers

that spend countless hours taking care of everyone but themselves. Are they heroes or self-sacrificing martyrs? This description is an example of a dominant archetype being extreme. If we are always caring for others and putting ourselves last, what will happen? We will become angry and feel resentful. And if we remain unaware, we will not know why we are experiencing these negative feelings. A caregiver can quickly become a victim to their archetype. This is yet another reason why it is essential to make conscious decisions and choices for our lives.

A healthy and balanced caregiver can feel proud and accomplished by their contributions. They have already filled themselves up with a healthy sense of self and want to share their gifts.

A dominant Warrior archetype can be a fighter. This state may transfer an intense energy to others that can exhaust them. Like the caregiver archetype, the Warrior can feel resentful too, because, hey—they are carrying the world on their shoulders to save us all. Without conscious thought, any self-sacrificing extremes can be powered by unnecessary responsibility. They can also feel victimized by their own unconscious choices.

Healthy Warriors use their laser focus to accomplish and contribute. They also feel proud of their accomplishments.

- Which archetype do you identify with? There are many!

- Do you have a dominant archetype?

- Would you like to diminish a certain trait?

- Do we want our CEO or Warrior to show up at home?

- Is it healthy to be a self-sacrificing caregiver filled with angst?

- What is the best way for you to show up for your family, work, community?

These questions can be relationship savers. Does a child want or need a Warrior showing up or to experience a loving, understanding, and compassionate parent? What does your spouse need and want?

Bob wanted to reengage with the Magician/Leader part of himself as well. The engaging, creative, fun, and magical part that doesn't give a hoot about his phone, technology, email, or anything other than seeing and enjoying his loved ones. Bob decided consciously that this part of him brings more joy to his family. His Warrior, which can move mountains by day, can also wear people out if not given a rest. Good to know! It turns out that his Magician allows others to feel good about themselves as well.

Bob's Magician allows him to be more creative and freer of personal restrictions like shyness, inhibitions, and introversion. When his Magician is active, it increases Bob's energy and confidence and brings him a feeling of sheer happiness. This part of him creates a contagious energy that encourages others to feel this happier too.

The Magician is all-knowing. He/she has an abundance of hidden and uncanny knowledge. Bob feels that this is when he is at his most giving, most loving, most available, and most authentic.

When Bob came to coaching, he wanted to know, "Where do I go from here? Who am I? What do I want? Do I want to stay married? How did I get to this place?"

Bob's journey continues. Re-engaging with his Warrior and Magician has given him insights into patterns that have brought him to some of his highest highs and lowest lows. He is clear about how he showed up in his business and with his wife and family.

He and his wife are moving forward with their marriage while simultaneously being united with their family goals. They are doing great now. They know that they can meet their needs within their marriage or outside of it. They believe that their children will do well with two conscious parents focusing on their growth and wellbeing. Their love for each other has grown with many realizations. They each have human needs to fill, goals to accomplish, and parts of themselves they want to bring forth!

Bob's work with his archetypes further helped him to solidify his sense of purpose. He consciously chooses his marriage and family and uses his gifts to live a vibrant and prosperous life.

Carol's Journey: Caregiver Archetype

Carol is a talented artist, wife, and mother of three. She lives in a cold climate that she hates. She rarely finds time for the thing that lights her up: her art. Carol desired to have a conversation with her Caregiver archetype.

This role was modeled by people that earned her respect when she was growing up. It came easy to her, and she usually took care of everyone in her circle. Now she found herself quick to anger and often confused. She also was experiencing headaches and fatigue. It seemed that she either had no expectations for others and had given up, or she had too many expectations and overwhelmed the people in her life. She came to coaching to find balance and to believe in herself once again. Why was she confused? Where does the caregiving end and Carol begin?

> *We can ask ourselves what the motivations are behind our archetypal patterns. Are they healthy or needy?*

If they are demanding and needy, we will end up tiring ourselves and others. It can be like being with a perfectionist or a control freak that has gone mad—no fun at all! The more Carol gave, the more she drained her energy and, unwittingly, the energy of others. This result is antithetical to what she wanted. She wanted and expected appreciation and love for her acts of kindness and sacrifice.

People can give repeatedly—until it becomes an unappreciated expectation. An expectancy may have the opposite effect of helping people. In some cases, it can even weaken their growth. It is not until something goes off the rails that circumstances are questioned. We want to give, but we also need to receive—balance is always the goal.

Carol found that she didn't have healthy boundaries. When we spoke with her Caregiver, Carol learned that she was always *looking* for love and acceptance instead of *feeling* love and acceptance! Being the Caregiver temporarily brought her those feelings as well as a sense of significance.

Carol asked her Caregiver to provide for others only when Carol felt well herself, and she consciously chose to do so. She understood that she doesn't need to work so hard to earn love, acceptance, and significance; it is already a part of her. Wow, was she already worthy?

Because the Caregiver role came easily to her, she had accepted it. The dilemma came when Carol realized that it was at a level that was affecting her own health and happiness. This negative result from constant good deeds came as a surprise to her, but as we asked questions of her archetype, the reason for this role choice became apparent. It is an innate strength. Perhaps her purpose in life! The Caregiver part of her is intelligent, insightful, and passionate in the healing of others. Carol didn't see these innate strengths as her gifts—until she did this work.

Because there can be a more nefarious side to every archetype, Carol wanted to find a productive way to find balance for this pattern in her life. Carol asked the Caregiver part of herself to care for *her*, to help heal and stabilize her first. She now had an awareness of how setting boundaries is a good thing and an understanding that it could be a deliberate choice when she brings forth this superpower for others. When we consciously choose where our efforts go, we rarely feel resentment or anger. We are much more apt to feel confident and proud.

Carol thanked her Caregiver for the talents that it brought to her life. She acknowledged this part of herself and feels proud of the skills she can share with others. She asked her Caregiver to help her set healthy boundaries and that it shows up in a balanced, conscious, and self-confident way.

She aimed to:

- Create a comfortable environment to sketch and paint.
- Set boundaries.
- Get paid for her services.
- Find balance in the give-and-take of life.
- Feel joyful and powerful.

Michael's Journey: Leader Archetype

Michael seemed to be drifting through life and always looking for a way to avoid responsibility. His mind was always running while he was standing still. He wanted to progress in life, particularly in his career, yet he continually put the brakes on. His go-to was to be just "good enough." This meant doing the bare minimum to maintain his job—but not to excel, grow, or to let a promotion even enter his mind. Bob knew that if he allowed himself to grow, he would have more responsibility. He might have to use more energy and stretch. He already felt that his life was too hard.

He had a real dilemma. In the pit of his stomach, he knew he was holding himself back from success. Yet, he wanted success! But it turns out that he didn't want to fail more. He didn't want to compete and take the chance of losing. He also feared being in the spotlight/seen. If he maintained "good enough," he could still face himself. However, liking himself was a different matter altogether. His energy was low. His health was spotty. His attitude to those around him was flawed.

Michael's efforts only went to what he knew he could do. You can't fail when you already know the answers. He lived vicariously through his family and friends' accomplishments and their hard-earned reputations.

But he came to coaching. Proactive people come to coaching! He had a desire for much more marinating in the pit of his stomach. He's a smart man who knew there was a better way. We first did the clarity work. We then moved onto strength work—and like Bob, soon he remembered his accomplishments. Michael was in a place of feeling hopeful when we started the Archetype work.

He wanted to speak to his Leader. This archetype was a smart choice. Michael knew that a leader leads! That he would be different after this work and a change in routine was usually outside of his comfort zone. Formerly he didn't take any risks—he was a master at controlling his "good enough" space. But this place of certainty (comfort zone) was an unrewarding place to stay and becoming painful.

The reason why this work is so effective is that we can feel the truth of our archetypes. We instinctively and unconsciously know that we have different parts of ourselves. When something feels truthful, the impact of the work can create a shift in a person quickly.

It wasn't Michael's Leader that brought him to this good enough point. He had let his Leader part slip away when he felt comfortable enough with his life. He didn't have any plans for further growth. He had reached a set point! Now he was bored. He knew he could create more—but there was fear! We both knew that his revisiting his Leader archetype was the part of Michael that could help him to find the motivation to move forward.

He now had to re-integrate his Leader. By staying conscious of it, he was able to adjust to his Leader part again quickly. He said, "Feels like a long-lost old friend." He created an extensive list of how his Leader had helped him during college when Michael had chosen to call on him more times than he could count!

We talked about why he got stuck and what payoffs he received by not moving forward. Michael felt it was now too painful for him *not* to act. He thanked his Leader for all the many years of help and asked him to stay present and available. He felt ready to grow in his career and realize his potential.

He aimed to:

- Talk to his supervisor.
- Offer to take on more responsibility.
- Ask for a pay increase.
- Celebrate!

He's now swinging for the fences and is on his way to growing past "good enough!"

Reflection

We change when it becomes almost impossible not to. We can get beat up, worn out, and even anxious by staying too long in our comfort zone. It is an oxymoron. We stay in a comfort zone to feel safe—to ward off the *I'm not good enough*—and in doing so, we can become unhappy and unsatisfied! Knowing our Six Human Needs reminds us that we need variety, growth and to contribute our best selves.

We often believe that making a change is the hard part, but we don't know that! Change is inevitable. We hold onto jobs we hate, toxic relationships, limiting beliefs, money to feel safe—none of which ultimately fulfill us. It is like swimming against a mighty current.

Then if we receive the understanding that we must let go and allow the changes to happen, we can move forward. Once we do, it becomes more comfortable, like we are swimming with the current. We take the leap, do the best we can—and either get close, reach, or in many cases we will surpass our goals. Sometimes we even realize we want to change our goals along the way. Again, change is inevitable!

Going Deeper

Ask yourself if you feel owned by a specific pattern of thinking. Is there a pattern of behavior that is not allowing you to accomplish goals? If so, you could have been living with a negative thought pattern for a long time. Try this process to integrate consciousness and gain greater access to your emotionally limitless potential.

Exercise

Find a quiet space and think about/write down the answers to the following questions.

- What is your dominant archetype?
- Describe how this archetype has limited you.
- Describe what gifts this archetype has for you.
- Are there any archetypes with which you immediately identify?
- What quality or strength are they suggesting for you to incorporate into your life?

Next, look for mentors, both living and dead, that embody strengths that you identify as positive. Ask yourself what it would feel like to be like these mentors and imitate this likeness within yourself.

Find that authentic piece of you that resonates with a specific trait. If it resonates with you, it is already inside of you. This work can expand who you are. You can integrate these hidden, healthy, new, and more powerful patterns into your daily life.

Summary

Archetypal work shows us that we have ways of being more dominant than others and identifying with more than one archetype. We can also see dominant archetype patterns in others that are universal and timeless.

Understanding archetypes gives us knowledge of ourselves and others that can predict behavior and how we experience emotions. Once understood, our archetypes can be strategically strengthened or diminished.

Chapter 12

FACING A CRISIS

Introduction

Do difficult situations provide some of the best opportunities to change and grow?

> *Why is it that in a time of crisis, we can "morph up to a new level"? It's because we have no choice! Otherwise, we will be left behind, or worse.*

A crisis doesn't bring on the quiet, calm, slow-paced growth that you can barely feel. No, an emergency sharpens all our faculties. It is through a difficult transition that we end up more assertive, more confident.

Perhaps one of the most significant rewards of a crisis is the shedding of superficial thoughts: goodbye and good riddance external fears. And how quickly that can happen! I'm not playing around being shy and humble any longer—I don't have the time; I've got some work to do. If we are ever going to throw caution to the winds in life, it will almost certainly come via a crisis.

Jarod's Story

When you realize that you have lost everything that you have built, it can be devastating. Jarod's day of reckoning was a personal crisis that turned his world upside down.

He described himself as honest, perhaps to a fault, as well as hardworking, compassionate, and insightful. He was not bragging; these were well-known strengths of his. For decades he brought these traits into work with him each day. He supported his colleagues and the goals of the company they all worked for. He took his stewardship role seriously. At home, he parented hard and tried to please and help everyone to meet their needs.

He was busy. He was responding. He was also successful—so he stayed on autopilot.

Eventually, he was blindsided by a myriad of unseen forces. Jarod erroneously believed that, like him, his colleagues were working with the same kind of integrity. However, when those colleagues saw the sky darkening, instead of joining with Jarod to do the right thing, they ducked their heads. His assumption that people would do their parts with equal integrity was proven to be a mistake.

He hadn't considered his co-workers' fears or the depths of their ambitions to succeed. He felt betrayed.

He wanted to be liked and go along with things, too. It certainly would have been an easier path for him to follow. He wanted to feel safe, trust his colleagues, and be supported. However, his values rose above his need to be liked.

Jarod was the kind of guy that could make his accomplishments appear easy. They weren't, but that was the impression that he gave. This led his higher-ups to both appreciate and fear him. When he was accomplishing his work goals it could make his colleagues and boss happy—or not so happy if they happened to be insecure. It was a balancing act and one that he didn't have the skills for.

The stress of holding things together for himself, his colleagues, and the organization took its toll. He worked there long enough to pass the torch to those brought in for damage control. He then became a scapegoat as colleagues maneuvered themselves into further safety. Some became ostriches and buried their heads to ignore the dysfunction that surrounded them.

People have a built-in set point of what they will allow. Jarod had reached his limit, and everything fell apart for him! He paid dearly for his lack of awareness.

He didn't initiate this change. He couldn't make it unhappen, but he also couldn't let his potential be unmet.

Most of us have felt the sting of betrayal at some point. Because Jarod had been so blindsided, he asked himself, "Can I trust myself, my instincts, at all?" He wondered if this awareness overload he was dealing with could be compared to the dark night of the soul. He did feel like he was in mourning. But what was he mourning? Jarod believed his only choice was to lick his wounds:

- He pondered the meaning of his life.

- He took long walks in nature.

- He read books by thought leaders.

- He had a lot of history to look back on.

- He thought about what liberty and the pursuit of happiness could/would look like for him.

- He pondered all his relationships and what they meant to him and what he meant to others.

Jarod lost his ego (or made excellent friends with it!). He lost layers of protection that he had built over the years—reputation, some friends, beliefs, a title, even his income, and his sense of balance.

Is your ego you?

We know our thoughts are not us. So, is what we do to protect our ego, trying to protect who we are? Who we think we are? Or who we want to be? If we become stripped of our accomplishments and ego—are we still worthy? Jarod did this deep dive into self-development work because he was forced to. He felt battered and bruised and wrung out. When you are in this place, you can fight, freeze, or flee. Or you can do a strategic climb out—a rebirth and transformation of sorts.

His efforts were to reconcile his present existence with where he had been and who he had been. Jarod started finding opportunities in the current moment. What changes could he make? What did he want now?

With all this questioning, Jarod started to get some answers. He learned viscerally that he was indeed human and allowed to be so. He had faults, flaws like everyone else, and that is okay. Everyone has their lost moments, and he indeed was having his. Now it became time to take steps to put himself back together again.

As we began, Jarod was able to state already, "I know what I don't want." This gave him the ability to ask himself, "So, what do I want now?" And because he was finally quiet for long enough, Jarod heard a little voice answer, "More, so much more than you ever wanted before." This led to the realization, "Oh boy, here we go." A mind, body, and spirit transformation were coming for Jarod, whether he liked it or not!

We created five non-negotiable daily rituals as a starting point for Jarod.

Morning:

- Coffee, quiet time, listening-to-self time, journaling thoughts, setting priorities as his day-starter.

Throughout day:

- Increase water intake.
- Double vegetable intake, all meals.
- Exercise 15-30 minutes morning and afternoon.
- Take five action steps daily towards meeting his goals.

Jarod's thriving. He now believes that what materialized to create his crisis was meant to happen.

Many of us need more than a little nudge to move on to our next chapter. Jarod ended up changing his career entirely and now focuses on growth. His business colleagues are like-minded and mission-driven people. He feels inspired daily and revels in the shared camaraderie and support. They are all respectful of each other's goals. He sees new opportunities everywhere he looks. It is as though the entire world has opened to him. And why not? We deserve nothing less! He is grateful that he could become aware of his choices and pivot many of his thoughts and actions.

Hindsight is a beautiful thing; it can also be cruel and sometimes makes us cringe. Jarod came out of his crisis happier and more aware than he had ever been. I asked him if he'd like to go back, do what he was doing, work with the people he was working with. He gave me a resounding no. His change in direction became the gift that he keeps on giving not only for him but for those that mean the most to him.

I asked what his most significant lessons were, and he

was quick to say, "The importance of being present, and that I should take the time to reflect on how I am showing up and contributing. I don't want to just respond to the circumstances around me. I want to maintain an awareness of myself and the people in my inner and outer circle. Now, I stop and check in to ask myself what action steps will take me to where I want to go. Plus, I make plans to have fun!"

We go through life being cautious. We are careful about this, fearful of that—and all that ends abruptly when a crisis arises.

In critical situations, we will no longer fear whether we are good enough, whether we are an imposter, whether our voice matters, or whether we are "keeping up with the Joneses." A crisis chases away these and similar Gremlins with which our ego can continually challenge and punish us.

In difficult situations, our Leader and Warrior parts of ourselves arrive and tend to supersede all the others. There is nothing like a good old-fashioned real-life crisis to light a fire under us! And once we get through one, we won't look at life in the same way. We will have grown into our power and become so much more resilient. A scratch on a car, a broken window, a child's tantrum, a glass of spilled milk, or a late house payment will not a crisis make.

Jarod's personal crisis was caused by the loss of his former lifestyle and all that he knew, had built, and created. His income, title and ego were at one time indistinguishable from who he is. He is Jarod, the cake, and what he does and what he contributes, is the frosting.

A crisis is a time of great difficulty, danger, and intense stress. Circumstances can become acutely real to us when we come face to face with a life-and-death situation. When political storms rage. When financial ruin becomes a reality. A threat to you or a loved one's health, environmental changes, and rampant violence—these are some crisis scenarios that we can face. There are more—there will always be more. They can cause our priorities to change in an instant.

Our life experience has taught us that we can create a new normal when necessary. We are resilient!

As always, we must believe in ourselves. Resilience-building isn't easy. It's hard work and a necessary life process. A child's resilience also grows during their challenging times—and by watching how their role models face adversity.

How can we call upon the strength we need in the most challenging of times? By calling on our accumulated resilience. It gives us the capacity to recover quickly from difficulties. Though it doesn't solve problems, it helps us face situations directly. The more stable and confident we are, the better we can keep our wits about us (or find them faster) and adapt to a new and sometimes frightening situation.

We can't erase sadness, worry, or fear. It seems to me those feelings are an innate part of life. They each have a unique place in our existence and teach us many lessons. It is during tough times, not the easy times, when we learn how to be resilient.

Going Deeper

Reality check: If a door has closed for me:

- What entry is available to me now?
- What can I make happen?
- Who can I partner or collaborate with to make things better?
- How do I want to show up?
- Or perhaps most importantly, how *can* I show up? What am I made of—what is my mettle? What are my superpowers? I know that I have them. Have I been hiding them until the time is perfect for pulling them out?

When is the right time?

> *In coping with life experiences, haven't we already been resilient? We may not have acknowledged it consciously for what it is, and there may lie the answer to how to call upon strength when the need arrives!*

We are familiar with the terms fight, flight, or freeze. These responses are natural results of different levels of threats and how we handle certain kinds of anxiety.

- Fight when the risk seems beatable.
- Flight when you have the advantage to escape.
- Freeze is the last resort and can kick in automatically.

Resilience helps us to recognize when we are in our natural survival mode response. Does the situation call for the response we are delivering? We can then take the appropriate steps to ground ourselves to see the situation clearly.

We are not one-dimensional people. As we know, there are many parts to each one of us. Sometimes in life, we must call in the big guns! One reason archetype work is so enlightening in coaching is that it can reveal certain aspects of how we think and respond. My clients enjoy getting reacquainted with parts of themselves that they have either neglected or forgotten. Some excellent empowerment work happens when we reestablish contact with our Leader, Warrior, Goofball, Teacher, Lover, and more.

Resilient people can find hope in difficult situations, while those without resilience tend to freeze or get stuck by circumstances. Hope comes from opening our minds to new possibilities. We understand that our fears are in place to keep us safe.

However, we should also continually ask ourselves whether our fears are diminishing our dreams. If

192

so, they are unhealthy and unnecessary roadblocks. Simple as that!

Reflection

Jarod experienced a crisis that changed the trajectory of his life. He didn't plan it, he didn't see it coming, and he did not want it. But, once he was in it, the circumstances demanded his attention because the situation affected every area of his life. He already had many life experiences that had given him the resilience to face this adversity.

Through his own reflection, he was able to tap into parts of himself that had been *dormant but are always available*—his Leader and Warrior made an appearance and helped him create a new, exciting, and more empowering path to follow. He used his wisdom from lessons learned to strategically create an approach that which brings him more joy and satisfaction.

Summary

We all fear a crisis, but unfortunately, they are part of the human experience. There are many kinds of crisis: being robbed, harassed, assaulted, divorce, facing illness or death, or losing your job.

Sometimes a crisis can be triggered by internal stressors such as depression with negative self-talk. Then there are natural environmental disasters, epidemics, pandemics that will demand our attention. Adversity produces a powerful energy that releases tremendous potential in us. The resilience we have already becomes compounded from rising above life's challenges. This emotional strength and the wisdom gained can be consciously used as a guide to repeatedly overcome future obstacles and up-level all aspects of our lives.

Chapter 13

MOVING FORWARD

Introduction

Have any chapters, stories, or processes resonated with you? Anything calling to you? Have you worked out what's holding you back? Most importantly, are you ready to make the changes to bring you more joy and the desired results?

The tale of the elephant and the rope

I love this story for the lesson it brings. Not that I would ever want an innocent animal trapped and unable to live its best life. I feel the same about people for the very same reasons.

There are traps, and then there are traps!

The story of the baby elephant is that he was tied daily to a stake. He would pull and tug at that rope that bound his ankle to the stake to free himself. It was useless.

He was too small, it was too hard, and try as he might, he couldn't break free. He lost all hope, and he finally gave up.

As the years went by, he grew to be massive in size and more majestic. He got more powerful too, but he had long ago been conditioned to believe that he was stuck. He would no longer even try to break free. He did not know that the ropes that bound him as a young elephant had NO power over him anymore.

How could he know? His conditioning had become his truth.

Failure is part of growth; failure could be the most important part of our learning. Even so, we cannot go through our lives focused on our failures. Each failure is a lesson that brings valuable knowledge for the next effort.

The elephant was conditioned from his failures to break free when he was young and unequipped. Had the binding become a comfort zone? Had he only known that if he tried *one more time* he could be free.

Like the elephant in this beautifully written empowerment tale, people can remain stuck by their previous conditioning.

> *Failures are just lessons that inform growth. Growth is one of our human needs. We must keep trying!*

Had the elephant been unrestrained in his natural habitat (free from Gremlins) as he deserved to be, he could have naturally felt his strength and majesty. He would learn his lessons from the other elephants, the environment, and his own life experiences.

He might happily and sometimes foolishly fall into mud puddles and get stuck. If he needed help, the older elephants would come to his rescue. He'd learn from these experiences. There would be no need for guilt, anger, or shame for getting stuck! The results would be a natural, uninterrupted life lesson.

The next time, he could gauge the mud puddle and decide what to do based on his acquired skills and experience. Then the day would come that he too would help the other young elephants, the ones that found themselves stuck as he once had been. The knowledge gained from experience becomes wisdom shared.

Contribution is another one of our human needs. Where does the courage to expand our minds, bodies, and spirits come from anyway? Is there some universal energy pulling us to expand our minds, grow, and then contribute?

Babies taking those first steps are compelled to do so. They are not afraid; they are fierce. It doesn't matter how many times they fall—they still get up!

Firefighters running into a burning building are courageous. They know the risk, are afraid but use their skills and experience to save lives, homes, and more.

Do you remember the joy that you felt when you learned to read, ride a bike, swim, dive, catch a ball, drive a car? All things that we once celebrated! They are procedural memories now. You do not have to try to remember how to do any of them—they are now a part of you. Do you remember the excitement felt by accomplishing these feats? The nerves, the challenge, the variety—the falling and the rising again—the success?

Seeing mental traps for what they are is the beginning of their demise. Notice if you are emotionally tied up anywhere. Ask yourself how and when these ties became compounded and constricting in your life. Assess them now for what they are. That is what we must do to make a positive change. Look to see where the ropes have frayed and stretched from your acquired experiences and earned knowledge. The threadbare ones are ready to break. Now, with trust in yourself, find that weakest rope and break free from it. Then move onto the next challenge and so forth.

Reflection

What was once true for the baby elephant was no longer true once he had grown, but he remained stuck in the old paradigm/conditioning/story. How can you make sure that doesn't continue in your life?

Question your current circumstances. Look at yourself objectively and with love. What old pattern is holding you back? Are you thinking empowering thoughts? What are you moving towards?

The mental ties and boundaries that you created may have served you well at one time. They probably kept you safe and were a great coping mechanism for life challenges. You may have been very smart to erect them *then*, but they are no longer needed now. So, you can thank them and send them on their merry way. It is time to follow your wisdom.

There comes a time in a person's life when they decide to stand in their truth or not stand in it. I'm not referring to decisions about career choice, education, which house to buy, or raising a family—although those are important decisions, for sure.

I'm referring to decisions about you as a person and how you will choose to show up for yourself when:

- You know that you are good enough and always have been!
- You don't care if another thinks your choices are foolish.
- You know you are not a fraud.
- You know that you have gifts to share.

When you know better, what then? Can we turn our backs on ourselves?

Going Deeper

Each section of this book is intended to resonate with clarity, growth, and purpose. You are doing this work for a reason. You are being purposeful in claiming your power by using your truth and strategies to create your life. You are looking for confidence and the freedom it gives, to let the fear of "not being enough" melt away.

Why not read through each chapter again, review your answers to the exercises, and consider your takeaways? Make a note or maybe even an inspirational poster for your home or workspace and revisit these lessons regularly—or at least until that new sense of belief in yourself becomes your new normal.

Exercise

Journaling can be a great source of finding clarity and healing. You can pour out your feelings of pain, hurt, guilt, and betrayal when you journal. Having your emotions on paper will help you to visualize your situation; you can add to it over time and re-read it often to see your progress. The objective is to feel less pain and fear and more freedom, lightness, and peace within yourself as you purge negative and limiting thoughts.

Summary

Thank you for reading *Strength Becomes You*. When you began to read this book, I believe that you wanted to live with more confidence and joy. I believe you became tired of living any other way.

My sincere wish is that you found something within these

pages that you know was written just for you. Something that gave you a realization that will motivate you to make one positive change in your life. One change will ignite even more changes. You will be affecting not only your life, but others' lives as well. This book is about building a case of support for people to believe in themselves, to never forget who they are, what they deserve, and all that they can accomplish.

We are living in interesting times for sure! The world is evolving at an incredible pace. I expect each generation believed that about the time they lived as well. They were the people for their time. And we are the people for our time. The connectedness of the global community, societies' structures, the technology, the way we learn—support others. We are on this fast-paced adventure together. People must evolve too and leave behind what does not serve them or others.

You have a purpose, perhaps more than one, and your contributions can bring you and others joy.

As we begin to climb out of the messy mud puddles of our lives, we need to remember how close we are to succeeding. One more tug from the elephant and he would be free. You too are always just one try away!

With that all said, I want to ask you one final question. The most spectacular, awesome, significant question ever asked!

So, what now?

Whatever your answer, I wish you an abundance of health, happiness, vibrant growth, and inner peace on your journey through life.

As you move forward, I suggest that you make a pledge with yourself that after one year, you'll return to this book and see how far you've come. If you need a little "fine-tuning," review what's here and then begin traveling again toward the life you deserve. Remember that *Strength Becomes You!*

References and Reading List

- *Think and Grow Rich* by Napoleon Hill
- *Man's Search for Meaning* by Victor Frankl
- *When Bad Things Happen to Good People* by Harold S. Kushner
- *Re-Awaken the Giant Within* by Anthony Robbins
- *Daring Greatly* by Brene Brown
- *The 15 Invaluable Laws of Growth* by John Maxwell
- *The Power of Now* by Eckhart Tolle
- *A New Earth* by Eckhart Tolle
- *The Four Agreements* by Don Miguel Ruiz
- *The Secret* by Rhonda Byrne
- *The Road Less Traveled* by M. Scott Peck
- *A Return to Love* by Marianne Williamson
- *How to Win Friends and Influence People* by Dale Carnegie

- *The Purpose Driven Life* by Rick Warren
- *Webster's Dictionary* by Merriam-Webster

The best way to connect with me is via my email Kathy@Quintessential-Coaching.com or my website **www.quintessential-coaching.com**. I'll do my best to respond. I look forward to our new friendship.

Acknowledgements

First, I want to thank my very special person, my husband Norman, for his continued and unfailing love, support, and understanding during my pursuit of writing *Strength Becomes You.*

To our children Norman, Bethany, and Allison. You each share your own special brand of magic with the world and make it a much better place. You have our hearts. Thank you for being your unique selves.

For our grandchildren, Emma, Julia, Brayden, Catherine, Caroline and Caine, whom we love so dearly and enjoy almost too much! We pray that you will find your own special brand of magic—you are well on your way—and that your world is always a good one.

To my sisters, Linda and Laurie, two of the finest, funniest, and most compassionate women that I know. May we continue to laugh, sing, and dance—and never give a hoot who's watching.

For my sisters' husbands, Larry, and Harry. Each, the embodiment of Father Christmas—pillars of good cheer, giver of gifts and the safety of home. Two regal, strong and kind men.

To my friends, colleagues, mentors, and supporters, please know that your encouragement and input have made the publishing of this book possible. It really does take a village!

Professional collaborations become successful when all involved are willing to bring their talents for what they do best. I owe a tremendous amount appreciation to the following people for doing just that!

Thank you to Kim Carr for bringing a myriad of publishing talents to my initial draft of this book and to my children's book series The Adventures of Quint the Bookmobile.

Thank you to the outstanding editing team of Lisa Tynan, Doris Siu, and Lin White for sharing their expertise of the written word and phrase—from a punctuation change here to an insight over there.

There was much brainstorming for the title of this book, and I'm grateful to Lisa Tynan for envisioning the one that stuck.

A heartfelt and deep sense of gratitude for the talented and exceedingly professional formatter Lin White. Yes, it really did come together.

A warm thank you to Strategic Branding Expert, Edna Dratch-Parker, for the concept of depicting a breaking through, with just a picture—take a beautiful daisy, the flower of hope and new beginnings, have it burst through its challenges with the strength to become all that it is meant to be.

I'd like to express my appreciation to book cover designer Lance Buckley for bringing our vision to life with the perfect combination of artistry and professionalism. In the end—we have a beautiful book cover that tells a story.

Finally, I wish to humbly thank my clients for sharing their perspectives, life stories, and development journeys with me. Your bravery and trust in stepping out of your comfort zones with such immense integrity and poise continue to inspire me daily. "Why not you?" "Strong, like tree!" "Now, just flick that Gremlin away!" And never forget— "You've got this!"

Made in the USA
Middletown, DE
09 February 2022